FROM FRAMEWORK TO FREEDOM

A History of the Sister Formation Conference

Marjorie Noterman Beane, Ph.D.
Loyola University Chicago

With a foreword by Margaret Fitzer, SSL
Executive Director, Religious
Formation Conference

UNIVERSITY
PRESS OF
AMERICA

Lanham • New York • London

Copyright © 1993 by
University Press of America®, Inc.
4720 Boston Way
Lanham, Maryland 20706

3 Henrietta Street
London WC2E 8LU England

Library of Congress Cataloging-in-Publication Data

Beane, Marjorie Noterman.
From framework to freedom : a history of the Sister Formation
Conference / Marjorie Noterman Beane ; with a foreword by
Margaret Fitzer.
p.   cm.
Includes bibliographical references.
1. Sister Formation Conference—History.   2. Monasticism and
religious orders for women—Education—United States—History—
20th century.   I. Title.
BX4210.5.B43   1993   255'.9'006073—dc20   93–19044 CIP

ISBN 0–8191–9125–6 (cloth : alk. paper)

The paper used in this publication meets the minimum requirements of
American National Standard for Information Sciences—Permanence
of Paper for Printed Library Materials, ANSI Z39.48–1984.

DEDICATION

To the Women Religious of America
who formed the movement this book chronicles.

ACKNOWLEDGEMENTS

Special acknowledgement is made of the American women religious, leaders in the Sister Formation Conference, who gave the author their time and encouragement and shared their insights about religious life and the changes they experienced during the years covered in this study.

Gratitude is given for the opportunity to work in numerous archival collections that house the written and pictorial history of this movement and, in particular, the Department of Special Collections and University Archives, Marquette University. It is here that the Sister Formation Conference/Religious Formation Conference Archives are stored.

Finally, the support and encouragement of many at Loyola University Chicago helped to make this publication possible.

Marjorie Noterman Beane

Chicago, Illinois
February, 1993

TABLE OF CONTENTS

DEDICATION
ACKNOWLEDGMENTS
TABLE OF CONTENTS
FOREWORD
INTRODUCTION

FOREWORD

Today terms like Operation Bootstrap and Operation Airlift sound like U.S. government descriptions for troop deployment in some part of the globe. To those schooled in the benefits of the change Operation Bootstrap and Operation Airlift brought about for American women religious, they frame a story to be told and known to the beneficiaries of the foresight and planning that they implemented. Marjorie Noterman Beane tells such a story in her book, *FROM FRAMEWORK TO FREEDOM: The History of the Sister Formation Conference.* She records a rich history that is unknown to many or forgotten in the avalanche of life's happenings or memory's capacity to forget. As someone whose own story as a woman religious began in the late '60's with the promise of Vatican II and its mandate for change in renewal, the grassroots movement that grew into the Sister Formation Conference is like discovering a limb of the family tree -- one you knew existed but only vaguely.

The Sister Formation Conference began in March of 1954 and inaugurated the beginning of a carefully planned education and formation of women religious for their ministries. The insights and social analysis that informed the Conference's efforts seem monumental when the obstacles are noted. At that time the only forum for gathering as women religious was as members of the National Catholic Education Association and that is where they began and they did not stop until they had been heard. Planned change was the gift of these women religious. With determination, dedication and devotion they identified needs and addressed them. The results were women religious trained as professional educators, hospital administrators, nurses, social workers and scholars in a systematic and opportune way. Those who led this movement were themselves highly educated women, often through part-time study, summer school and Saturday classes. They saw the need for something better. With accuracy they read the signs of the times in 1954 and correctly noted: that by 1971 more lay teachers than sisters would staff Catholic schools; the challenge of being a minority group in what were thought to be their own schools; lay people would need to adjust to this new situation and discover ways of financing Catholic schools; future planning was a necessity for survival. From the vantage point of 1993 that is an impressive list of reading the signs of the times.

As the current Executive Director of the Religious Formation Conference, the present day Conference that is the heir and beneficiary of the Sister Formation Conference, reading Marjorie Noterman Beane's book offers perspectives and learnings about the history of this Conference and religious life in this country in the 1950s through 1960s. Formation itself is an oft disputed term as it conjures up visions of molding that ignores the life experiences and overrides or ignores individual differences. It is noteworthy that it was chosen precisely because it addressed the total person. A necessary piece of history as "formators" search the thesaurus for a more accurate word. The planned change these women orchestrated is necessary still. Wise as serpents, they set about advancing the mission of Jesus in the world. They found support from Rome, offered model programs of formation for the world and prepared a large number of women leaders. One current study on religious life underlines the considerable need today to focus on determinants of the future. The tradition for doing so is apparent in these pages. If then, why not now? Hopefully interpretations for the road ahead. Those of us whose own history is caught in-between the story told in these pages and the present, are richer for knowing what has gone before.

Margaret Fitzer, SSL
Executive Director
Religious Formation Conference

INTRODUCTION

"It is necessary and important that this story be told." I have heard this comment many times from women religious and those interested in their history. So I began investigating and chronicling the history of the organization known as the Sister Formation Conference in 1986 when I was permitted to work among its early papers. I was interested in learning about the movement which became a catalyst of change within religious life. Its leaders fascinated me. I also knew that my own life had been affected by this organization.

I entered religious life after completing high school in 1964. Like other young women I anticipated a life of service to the Church and expected that training, both professional and spiritual, would be part of my education. Little did I realize that I was stepping into religious life during a time when subtle changes in long traditions of formation were beginning. Religious communities of women, influenced and supported by the work of the Sister Formation Conference, were searching for better ways to prepare their sisters for the apostolic work they would be doing. The method of allowing these women to enter classrooms and other work places without the same credentials as their lay contemporaries was deeply questioned.

The community I joined had decided upon and was implementing a plan that enabled new entrants to earn a degree before beginning their apostolic work. Therefore, I received my first two years of college education during my novitiate by attending classes at the junior college housed in the motherhouse. Then, as junior sisters, my group and I were sent to Marillac College in St. Louis, Missouri in order to complete our first degree.

Marillac College, open only to women religious, was owned and operated by The Daughters of Charity. This community welcomed the junior sisters of many communities to attend their college--a pattern repeated all over the United States as communities reached out to help one another.

While attending Marillac College, our living and learning environment was influenced by a wholistic approach to formation. Most of us were living in juniorate communities. Besides being full-time students, we were expected to volunteer our services as tutors, catechists, visitors to the sick and indigent; wherever we were needed in the St. Louis area. We were encouraged to join student clubs, student government, school plays, art projects, a school newspaper and magazine. In my graduating class of 1969, seventeen different religious communities of women were represented. We earned degrees in natural science, mathematics, American studies, biology, English, mathematics, French, psychology, history, nursing, theology, and sociology. We were prepared to be teachers, social workers and nurses.

Unless you were in religious life or were aware of the educational practices at the time, it is hard to explain how exceptional this educational experience was for many women religious and for their communities. For the first time many communities were allowing and encouraging their sisters to experience a college education as close to that of their lay contemporaries as was possible at the time. Not more than ten years before, most of these religious communities were patterning the education of their members after a "twenty year plan" of summer school sessions that allowed the sisters to get their first degree.

Those of us that earned a degree during these "enlightened" years were early recipients of an integrated educational experience won by the hard work and foresight of the leaders of the Sister Formation Conference. It was our generation that was thoroughly and professionally prepared for our work with the idea that we could then serve to the best of our ability.

I predict that when those who entered religious life before 1954 read this history, they will recognize the players in this book and the issues that brought about the Sister Formation Conference. They will also know on a personal level what it meant to spend many years earning a first degree. For those of us who entered religious life after the beginnings of the Sister Formation Conference, this history will tell of the sacrifice and vision of religious women in communities across America and how their crusade gave us the opportunity to be women of the Church in the Modern World. The work and efforts of the Sister Formation Conference Movement have been unheralded, yet this organization has radically changed the course of the education of American women religious.

I am grateful that the opportunity has now come to share the story of the Sister Formation Conference. Let it stand as a tribute to the faith-filled and hard-working lives of American women religious who have always been ingenious in their service to the Church. It is my hope that as you read *FROM FRAMEWORK TO FREEDOM,* you will agree "that it is necessary and important that this story be told."

CHAPTER I   TIME OF CRITICAL SHIFTS   1948-1954

FROM FRAMEWORK TO FREEDOM: A History of the Sister Formation Conference was done in order to bring to light an area of American history that has received little attention; namely, the educational history of the American woman religious, and the place of the Sister Formation Conference in that history. In order to understand the Sister Formation Conference (SFC) in its entirety, this study of the movement is placed within a broad historical context that encompasses the directions and directives of the Church, the educational trends of the period, and the struggles and developments within American religious life during this time. This is a "new history"[1] that helps to put meaning into the changes that took place among American women religious during the years 1954-1964 by looking at their educational journey. To locate these women and this movement historically means to deal with "the paradoxes and the ambivalence of contemporary American Catholicism"[2] at a time when dependence, conformity, and institutionalized living were the marks of religious life. By the end of the period, these women were experiencing a new kind of responsibility, community building, and discernment.

The story of the Sister Formation Conference tells of the evolution of an idea that reached its own time. That idea conceptualized the American woman religious as an integrated woman, as a prepared professional, and as an embodiment of Church. The idea took shape as clear-sighted, American women religious fought consistently for the right to be professionally prepared for the work they sought to do in and for the Church. These women, not always supported by those they sought to work with and for, found their energy and strength in a cohesiveness among themselves and in a united vision of what was definitely needed to achieve this monumental goal.

The Sister Formation Conference was to be the enabling agent for the professional growth of American women religious. With its roots grounded in the workings of the National Catholic Education Association (NCEA), the SFC evolved from the Teacher Education Section of that same association. The

1

evolutionary birth of this women's movement was marked by critical shifts of thinking in the Catholic Church, in religious life, and in the field of education. Church documents, professional requirements, and the position of the women religious in America gave the founders of the SFC the energy needed to do the monumental task of pulling American women religious into the twentieth century and then preparing them for the twenty-first century. Advertently, the SFC spoke always of formation rather than just education. This choice of words indicated the deep and broad concern these women had for the total development of the religious woman in all aspects of her life, spiritual and intellectual.

The Church had asked for excellence in teaching and for highly prepared ministers able to meet the needs of the time. The year 1950 was an historical grounding point for women religious as Pius XII for the first time called an international meeting of the heads of religious communities (male and female) in order to urge a renewal in religious life that called for "theological education and professional credentials for those teaching and doing other professional work" and for "the elimination of outdated customs and clothing that estranged them from those they served."[3]   Another meeting in September 1951 for members of teaching communities was even more specific in its recommendations. Pius XII encouraged changes in the life-style of the active community so that the needs of the apostolate could be better met. More specifically, he asked that the teaching sister have the same professional training as her lay counterpart. There were other meetings, all aimed at calling attention to the need for professionalism in ministry. In 1954, Regina Mundi in Rome was approved as a pontifical institute of higher learning and a model "for training, education and formation of religious women in the sciences and disciplines."[4]

The Catholic Church in the American society of the 1950s, however, was fairly complacent. With a growth from twenty-eight million people in 1950 to forty-three million in 1963, Catholic institutions and services increased. The task of the woman religious at this time was that of serving the needs of the Church primarily in the capacity of teacher, nurse, or social worker. When the leaders of the SFC set out to create a systematic plan to revolutionize the training of women religious by emphasizing the necessity of integrated formation, they met with resistance. Bishops and pastors did not easily see the need to change a pattern that seemed to be succeeding so well.

Educationally, this era was caught in a revolution sparked by changing patterns and processes. Events such as the passage of the GI Bill, the rise of progressive education, and the news of Sputnik triggered a shift in emphasis in education. Facing the critical needs of the day, educators initiated a new surge toward teacher training that was linked with a call for educational reform. In 1946, the National Education Association set up a commission that was designed to carry on a number of activities that would stimulate and contribute to the advancement of standards that would result in the professionalization of teaching. Catholic schools were experiencing the height of their great expansion period. The sacrifices of the people, the directives of the Councils of Baltimore, the rendered services of women religious, and the guidance of pastors built the largest parochial system in the world. The dream of Catholics in America was to provide for their own people in a way supportive of their beliefs the same educational services available through the public system. The role of women religious in the Catholic educational system was not to be underestimated.

Religious sisters were the backbone of the Catholic educational system. Approximately 90,000 sisters were teaching in America at the time. When there was a call to examine the credentials of teachers in the United States, this included the credentials of the sister. As sisters began to seriously study their own situation, it became evident that an upgrading of professional credentials was not only necessary but imperative. Though this would put a severe financial burden on all communities and change patterns of formation, there was no other way to have prepared ministers. No longer was it enough to believe that God would supply with His grace what was lacking in the professional preparation of these women. This conflict of "grace of state" versus "professional competence" was significant. Within a short time, sisters across the United States came to understand that getting their first degree over twenty summers was no longer the best preparation for their work. Introduced into religious communities was an "equal opportunity" clause so to speak that would allow all to receive the same basic preparation.

In the late 1940s, sisters began working toward an organization that would help provide for the updating and professionalization of all sisters. Significant pioneer research was done concerning the proper professional training for sisters by Sister Bertrande Meyers, DC. In 1941, Sister Bertrande's dissertation entitled "The Education of Sisters" was published. In this work, she indicated that to educate a sister was to make her a better sister. After making an extensive study of educational practices among communities, Sister Bertrande made several recommendations. Sister felt that the problem of teacher education for sisters needed desperately to be addressed. She recommended that a plan for this education be worked on so that adequate training would take place. She believed that this training should take place within the spirit of each community. In order to do this, she felt that each community should organize its own junior college under the motherhouse so that the academic and professional training could be best coordinated with growth in religious life. The influence of Sister Bertrande's research is poignantly attested to by Sister Mary Emil Penet, IHM: "Your community pioneered in this work by permitting you to do the research which led to your dissertation, and every congregation in the country has been in its debt since then. . . .What is more, I feel personally that the real beginning of the Sister Formation movement must be dated to the publication of your book."[5]

The Sister Formation Conference worked toward structuring and promoting a total education that would insure a well-developed intellectual and spiritual life for women religious. Its leaders were charismatic and far-seeing. They labored at establishing communication within and among communities so that new ideas could be shared. They called for cooperation and planning among the leadership, formation, and academic personnel of each community. They foreshadowed the subsidiarity and shared authority concepts that developed after Vatican Council II. They sought and secured the approval of the Church. They contended with internal dissensions and polarity. Attempting to translate new ideas into actions was the challenge constantly before the SFC. To prepare women religious who would be competent, creative, and able to serve was always the goal. It is these labors, struggles, and achievements and their impact on American religious women that are documented in this study.

Teacher Education Section of the NCEA

Although sisters in every field of professional work would benefit from the efforts of the SFC, it was the desperate need of better preparation for sisters in the teaching profession that gave this movement its initial momentum. Only in the field of education were sisters able to begin their full time work with minimal professional experience and a "twenty year plan" to complete their educational degree. The "twenty year plan" was the term used to describe the way in which most sister teachers received their formal education. This plan would begin with varying amounts of education received in the novitiate, enough to prepare the sister for the classroom. The sister would then attend summer school for many summers to complete her first degree. This situation was true for all or most teachers, lay and religious, in public and in private systems, until the mid-1940s when a push was made to professionalize the field of education. It was the already educated women religious working for their own sisters who would win the case for allowing sisters to get their degrees before teaching. Sr. Josetta Butler, RSM, says:

> I would like to emphasize the role that the Sister Administrators in our Catholic Women's Colleges played in the development of the program in Sister Formation. Many of these administrators met frequently at the yearly meetings of educational associations, e.g., NCEA, North Central, American Council on Education, Association of American Colleges, etc. Often the main topic of discussion among these sisters was the realization of the necessity

to provide a college education for their sister teachers which when integrated with their religious formation would enable them to become competent religious teachers.[6]

These sisters working in colleges and universities met in the section of the National Catholic Educational Association [NCEA] designated the college and university department. The NCEA was organized into the six departments; major seminary, minor seminary, college and university, elementary, secondary, and superintendents. It was in the college and university department that a new concern was openly voiced in 1948; a concern that centered on the educational standards for the elementary and high school sister teacher, a concern foreshadowed by similar movements in the public sector.

It became more apparent to the college administrators that no longer would religious communities be able to assign young sisters to classrooms immediately following the completion of the novitiate (some of whom had not even finished high school). Natural aptitude and experience would not be sufficient. A formal general education beyond high school as well as professional training was needed. Another factor demanding this action was the rapid expansion of high schools. Soon high school teachers would be required to have a college degree and also to be certified to teach specific subjects. The SFC could become a tremendous force in showing the necessity for preparing our Catholic schools for accreditation and our sister teachers for certification.[7]

The 1948 assembly of the NCEA would be considering the challenge of the need for the greater professionalism of the Catholic educator. The National Catholic Educational Association could be termed the Catholic adaptation of the National Education Association. Founded in 1904, the NCEA provided the only organization which reached all levels of Catholic education and the only organization which could reach the Bishops' Committee on Education in the National Catholic Welfare Conference. Thus, this was the organization that people came to if they were Catholic and had an idea, a cause, a need. It was the only organization open to American women religious and their needs. Hence, there was absolute necessity for sisters to work through this organization and their corresponding dependence on this association to recognize the need for professional formation of the sister teacher.

National efforts to elevate teacher status in the public sector was evident. In July of 1946, the NEA established a National Commission on Teacher Education and Professional Standards, quickly known as TEPS, in order to responsibly upgrade and guard the professional level of teachers. Within a few years, as many as forty-three states were participating in the highly structured campaign to upgrade the standards in all areas of the teaching profession: recruitment, employment, promotion, evaluation, and in-service. Catholic educators too, felt called to improve standards in the Catholic educational system.   History was made at the 1948 meeting of the NCEA when, under the auspices of and within the college and university department, the Teacher Education Section was established and met for the first time. This section, organized through the efforts of the sisters in higher education, would give specific attention to the educational needs of sisters. According to the autobiography of Sister Madeleva Wolff, CSC:

> For years, a stubborn group of the college section of the national Catholic Educational Association had dreamed of, had asked for a section in the Association for teachers' preparation. Reasons for refusal now seem absurd. Then they were effective, final, and fatal. At the meeting of the Association in San Francisco in the spring of 1948, I [Sister Madeleva] asked for the last time that such a section be authorized and put to work. Approval was overwhelming.[8]

Brother Emilian, FSC, Provincial of the Christian Brothers and president of the College and University Department, called the meeting of nineteen priests, brothers, and sisters to order. Sister Madeleva was chosen as the temporary chairperson of the Teacher Education Section. That this group astutely perceived the particular needs of the time was evidenced by two resolutions that came from this meeting: that one executive session of the 1949 NCEA general convention be devoted to the needs of sisters and that the General Executive Board of the National Catholic Educational Association be requested to present to the Bishops of the United States the desire of the new Teacher Education Section to: "support them [the Bishops] actively and practically in requiring, implementing, and protecting adequate pre-service professional preparation and training for our religious teachers."[9]   It was imperative, Sister Madeleva noted as she brought this first meeting to a close, that all members of the group recognize their personal responsibility to foster the goal of the Teacher Education Section, particularly by bringing specified needs to the attention of priests and bishops. The specified needs centered on the education of young religious teachers with a consideration that the matter and manner of this education receive direction and authorization from the hierarchy specifically charged with this responsibility.

This group devoted to college and university concerns became the seedbed for interest in improved teacher educational standards for sisters because of a deep conviction of the need for quality in Catholic education. This conviction was linked with an abiding and haunting feeling that no real changes could occur in the Catholic educational system without raising the educational level of sisters. Two specific reasons for this concern which appeared to stand out above the rest were the interest of parochial teachers not to be outdone by their public counterparts and the interest of a select group of sisters in raising the professional standards of their own sisters.

The NCEA Convention of 1949 was again animated by the participation of Sister Madeleva, a legend in her own day. Sister Madeleva was a widely published poetess, author of nineteen books, extensive lecturer, and president of St. Mary's College, South Bend, Indiana for twenty-seven years. She founded the graduate school of sacred theology there in 1944, the first of its kind for women. Her two presentations were powerful and timely. In "The Preparation of Teachers of Religion," she emphasized three areas that would be used as platform points in speeches and as topics of research in the years ahead: that the religious habit did not automatically make the teacher, that there should be a conscious effort made to prepare lay people to teach religion, and that when sending sisters on for a degree, the quality of their education was important. It was a conference paper entitled "The Education of Sister Lucy,"[10] however, that became known as a classic presentation, the "turning-point" presentation in the early movement for sister formation. Sister Madeleva spoke clearly, precisely, and emotionally when she spoke of Lucy as the 1949 model of the religious teacher of the future. "Lucy" was the enthusiastic young person who outside of religious life would have worked for her degree and have been a successful educator but who, now, when called by God, faced the difficulty of having to teach without a degree, with only partial preparation. Sister Madeleva challenged the group of mother superiors and priest superintendents before her: "Because Lucy becomes a sister, does that mean she does not need to get her degree?" Sister Madeleva proceeded to answer her own question by stating that nothing could undermine a vocation more than lack of professional preparation. She was quick to point out the responsibility assumed by a religious community to train according to ability any young woman who entered. Sister Madeleva conceded that there would always be a great need for sister teachers and that this need could not be the deciding factor in determining how much education would be given to a woman before she began her apostolic work. Sister offered a final, forceful reflection:

> If all our religious communities begin this year to complete the education of our young sisters before sending them out to teach, practically all of the immediate generation will have their degrees and licenses in two or three years. After that, our teaching communities will have established this pattern of time and study

training. They will have the same number of sisters to send out each year, with this incalculable difference, that they will all be adequately prepared. Summer schools thereafter can be devoted to graduate work, particularly in theology, and Sister Lucy will still be "young Sister Lucy" when her teacher training has been complete. She will have the vitality, the enthusiasm, the quick mind and generosity of youth to give to her best years of teaching. How shortsighted, how stupidly extravagant we have been in squandering these![11]

The significance of Sister Madeleva's vision and challenge for women religious in America was that this particular vision and challenge was spoken publicly. Consciously or unconsciously, sisters were pleading for help to solve a situation that they could not remedy by themselves. Earlier studies had pushed for reform and action, but Sister Madeleva's challenge represented the beginning of a systematic plan to revolutionize the professional training of women religious. It is doubtful that any major superior was surprised at what she heard at this convention; she was only bewildered as to how to meet the new demands without a plan of some kind. For superintendents, a new demand for teacher training could only spell difficult days as the demands for teachers already exceeded the available number. "Sister Lucy had been admitted to college,"[12] Sister Madeleva would later write concerning the impact of this meeting.

At this same convention, some communities shared how they were attempting to meet the professional needs of their sisters. The educational plan for the sisters in the Diocese of Cleveland was explained along with the Ursuline Plan whereby all sisters were given at least a bachelor's degree before starting classroom teaching. The educational program of the School Sisters of St. Francis also demanded that their sisters have a degree before teaching. This type of sharing, of helping one another, was to become a hallmark among religious sisters in this movement and a sign of their solidarity with one another.

Another group that shared openly with sisters was the religious priests and brothers, who in many respects already had well established educational programs for their communities. It was a less conspicuous talk by Brother Emilian, FSC, that capped this session of the NCEA. His advice to provincials was both humorous and full of wisdom and showed the thinking of the day among male religious communities.

When the blow of your appointment falls, go to the Chapel for an hour of quiet, undisturbed prayer--it might be the last opportunity you will have for a few years. As you leave the Chapel, let your heart turn to stone and permit your head to follow suit. Cloak yourself with the hide of an antiquated walrus. Announce boldly that you will hold every candidate in training until he has received at least the bachelor's degree. Your plan will be loudly approved until there is need for a replacement which you cannot make without robbing the scholasticate. From that time on you may expect to lose friends, sleep, and orderly digestion. During the second term you have another duty to your congregation and to the cause of Catholic education in the United States. Announce your determination to educate all candidates up to and including the master's degree. At this point a long vacation is recommended. Criticism will be long and articulate. You can expect criticism. Hold to your plan and you will confer one of the finest favors possible upon your congregation. Your religious will gain as much spiritual profit from the added years as you hope they will advance professionally. Better far a small group of real religious with adequate professional training than a multitude of men clothed in the religious habit to whom the religious life and the science of education are mysterious tomes with uncut pages.[13]

At the NCEA Convention of 1950, members of the Teacher Education Section were again ready to spread the good news about education and were willing to work hard to change the traditions that had come to be known as the norm in teacher education. Familiar voices spoke again, this time at a meeting with the superintendents' department of the NCEA. At this session the philosophy that was to guide the Teacher Education Section was articulated by Msgr. Clarence E. Elwell, Superintendent of Catholic Schools, Cleveland, Ohio.

I conceive the purpose of this section to be to dedicate itself to the promotion of that high ideal of teacher preparation which is in consonance with the needs of the times, the best interests of Catholic education in this, our beloved land, and in keeping with the traditionally high standards of our Church.[14]

The quality of teacher education and the traditions of the Church were indeed the compass points of this movement for sister education. Quality Catholic education was the goal and two sets of pressures were setting up guidelines as to how to reach this goal. Outside pressure came from the growing certification demands, varying by state, which spoke clearly of the needs of the times. Internal pressure came from the desire to follow the directives of Church leaders and documents which spoke of the need for adequate preparation of teachers.

The discussions that pursued the articulation of the teacher-education philosophy centered on what kind of education for teachers was needed. The terms "general education" and "liberal arts" were interchangeably used, and a listener would perhaps have been hard pressed to know if he was at the NCEA or the NEA so similar were the discussions taking place. Aside from the frequent mention of the need of a strong foundation in religious education at the NCEA, both associations were battling with the concept of what it meant to be an educated person. The need to extend a complete education to sisters was finally being recognized; for, if the sister was to be effective in the classroom, she had to have the same, if not better, education than her lay counterpart.

While the two associations could dialogue about general education issues, the education problem of sisters was specific to the NCEA and the Teacher Education Section. There was not complete agreement as to the best practical way to understand the problem or how to solve the problem of setting new norms for teacher education. Several reservations against demanding a degree before teaching were voiced at the 1950 NCEA convention. Many believed that the young sister needed teaching experience before completing her education. Many felt that sisters should not have an uninterrupted education when forty-five percent of the public school teachers did not have degrees. Others thought education should take place only if perseverance was assured. What seemed like an insurmountable issue was the two-to-three-year time span when no young sisters would be going out to teach if this plan were put into effect. Finally, it was questioned how a professional education could be successfully integrated with the formation needed for religious life. It was this last reservation, the integration of the professional with the spiritual, that was to be the most difficult to work through and one that consumed the energy of the yet to be founded Sister Formation Conference. The new model of education was asking that the needs of the person be recognized along with the needs of the Church.

Cognizance of the fact that religious life at this time was viewed as a blend of the monastic and the active life perhaps answers the question as to why there would be fears connected with changes proposed to meet the adequate professional formation of the young sister. The ever-present cloud over the education of the sisters was the cloister traditions in religious communities. Sisters had to travel together, study together, eat together, dress differently from the laity, and read only certain books. The restrictions that were meant to foster a life devoted to God and neighbor were now causing difficulty in responding to the ministry demands of the day. As sisters advanced to education in colleges and universities, the concept of cloister isolation that had insured a protected but somewhat incomplete education had to fade away. The struggle involved in this transition was felt by the individual, by the religious community, and by the Church. Dependence, conformity, and institutionalized functionalism, once accepted as marks of religious life, were questioned at the same time that new pressures from within and from without were being experienced. Attempting to follow the call of the Church to reform, American women religious sought to use the tool of education as the means to making their life-style and work relevant to the needs of the day. Each community was faced with the hard decision of how to work new formation plans into their tradition and how to meet the costs of college educations. The university system needed to open to this group of women. Opportunities for sisters to enter higher education escalated as plans rooted in the need for intellectual and moral formation continued to develop.

The work done at the 1951 NCEA convention demonstrated that slow but deliberate progress was being made toward a stance for sister education. A resolution that a four-year degree program was needed for both elementary and secondary teachers and this, as a minimum, was passed at this convention. To carry out this resolution, members "urged that something be done to enlist the help of the hierarchy, superintendents, supervisors, and pastors in the employment of lay teachers as an essential means to make possible adequate teacher preparation for the Sisters."[15] Committees were formed to study certification requirements for both the states and the dioceses as these requirements were often the basic yardstick used to determine what courses were necessary for sisters. Further, deans of colleges and schools of education, superintendents and supervisors were invited to assist in the organization of effective teacher education programs, for they were aware of the educational norms of the day.

The previous forms of teacher preparation for Catholic American women religious were about to crumble. Economic pressures, the demand for teachers, and in-house educational systems had created the old system. Now, the training that had taken place in motherhouses under the guidance of trained fellow sisters would be replaced by a degree program. It was the average sister that this new program of education would help, for until this time, the sister of superior intelligence was usually the only one cultivated and she became almost encyclopedic in her knowledge. Each community followed its own pattern of education and few had all sisters earning a degree before teaching. It was the awareness of new trends in teacher certification and accreditation, however, that weighed heavily on those responsible for the education of the sisters.

Other needs were becoming apparent as this movement began to unfold--not only were lay teachers needed but adequate places of education were needed. Institutions of Catholic education, no matter when founded, were now struggling with the question of what was needed for a sound professional and spiritual formation for the teacher. If a degree was the need of the day and the curriculum provided for only the practical professional education, what kind of changes were needed and how these were to be made became the agenda of concerned women religious. It was these critical and mounting concerns that made religious women all over America ready to take gigantic steps for change in the next years.

The Survey

At the Kansas City NCEA convention April 1952, the next historic step in the crusade for sister education was taken. As a session of the Teacher Education Section, a panel had been assembled to discuss Pope Pius XII's document entitled "Counsel to Teaching Sisters." Four sisters spoke on the document's implications for sister education. They stressed that general education was needed for the prospective teacher's preparation and that the education of religious teachers was to correspond in quality and academic degree to the demands of the state. The capstone of the panel presentation was the talk of Sister Mary Emil Penet, IHM. After speaking a little on the new four-year degree program offered to all sisters of her community, she identified the difficulties of all teaching communities in maintaining an educational program. These difficulties were summarized as: limited time given to sisters to finish their degree, shortage of finances to cover the cost of the education, and lack of understanding of the needs and problems of the sisters in the field of teaching. Sister Mary Emil then proposed three solutions to these problems: that there be a uniform ratio suggested concerning the hiring of lay teachers to supplement the ranks of sisters as some left to get their degrees; that a study be made to determine how communities lacking in funds were to carry out the Holy Father's directives; and lastly, that there be some kind of organizational unity among motherhouses and colleges engaged in education in order to better understand the goals and current state of sister-education.

Sister Xaveria Barton, IHM, present at this session, explained how Sister Mary Emil came to be one of the speakers and gave her description of the session:

> So the upshot . . . was that Sister Mary Patrick was asked to come to the NCEA Convention in Kansas City. Sister Mary Patrick was ready to go out the door almost when she got word that her dearest sister was dying up in Minnesota, so she contacted Sister Mary Emil and said, "You go in my place." Sister Mary Emil prayed all the way to Kansas City. She said, "I can't get up and talk about our program. We're only a couple years old; it isn't tried and true enough." So she decided that she would talk about the need for consideration for the Sisters and that they were whole people and they had to have an integrated training in their spiritual and religious life, in their intellectual life and in their professional

life. That was the key. She made no bones of the fact that she had seen too much of the abnormal stress being placed on them, asking them to do things they were unprepared to do either in college or in the classrooms or the hospitals. But anyway, she stood up and made her speech. . . .Sister gave her little talk and there was a standing ovation from the Sisters. The superintendents stayed in their seats and looked angry, but Msgr. Voight--he was Cardinal Spellman's Executive Secretary for Education--was monitoring the entire program and once he got order back in the hall, superintendents sprang to their feet and said, "This is nonsense. Those Sisters are ready to go out. They're taught methods and such and such." As Sister Mary Emil described it when she came home, it was just a back and forth. The Sisters were angry too, you know, not name-calling but next to it. Emotions were sky-high, so finally Msgr. Voight said, "What I see is that there are two points of view and they can't be resolved without the facts. We need the facts. I recommend that there be an ad hoc committee formed from the membership of the Sisters to gather the data."[16]

The discussion that ensued went down in NCEA minutes as a "lively discussion from the floor. . . .There was a consensus of opinion that no religious community could solve these problems alone."[17] Monsignor John Voight, Superintendent of Catholic Schools in New York City, directed the discussions and encouraged that a specific study be done:

Well, if the Sisters need more salary, I'd like to see some statistics on just how much more, and what they are getting in various parts of the country. I suggest that we make some kind of survey of all these problems, so that we can bring this information to the attention of the Bishops.[18]

All kinds of objections were raised by the superintendents present as to why such a study would be impossible to do, chief among them being that there would be no one able to do it. The sisters quickly said that they would do it. A volunteer committee was formed outside the convention room and Sister Mary Emil was chosen to chair the group. The other members of this committee were Sister Mary Florence, SL, Sister Mary Richardine, BVM, Sister Gerard, OSF, and Sister Mary Basil, SSND. The purpose of the committee was to direct the work of conducting a survey regarding the current status of teacher education among sisters. Responses were to be accurate and detailed in order to better understand the needs and problems facing communities in providing for an adequate education to their sisters. Two things are to be noted here: not only was the problem of sister education now being openly studied, it was being studied with the approval of the most powerful Catholic Education group--the NCEA. If change was to occur in the educational pattern of sisters, it could happen only with the help and consent of the extended Church, i.e., the laity, clergy and other religious.

The sisters conducting the survey gave five reasons for the kind of research they would do:

1. Because the necessity that our Sisters be as well or better prepared than the demands of the STATE would require them to be was stated by His Holiness, Pope Pius XII, in his directive to the First International Congress of Teaching Sisters in Rome, September, 1951, and was reemphasized by our Holy Father at the meeting of Mothers General in Rome, September, 1952.

2. Because present overcrowded classrooms and pressure for teachers for new parochial schools and for expansion of those already in existence have resulted in Sisters' being placed in schools without minimum teaching preparation.

3. Because 33 of the United States at present require or have set dates in the very near future when a bachelor's degree will be necessary for any type of teacher certification.

4. Because--apart from other considerations--in those dioceses where salaries have not been increased sufficiently, present-day inflation causes many Religious Communities to be financially unable to meet the educational requirement of the STATE.

5. Because an additional two million pupils would like to be admitted to our schools but cannot by reason of the lack of teachers and schools.[19]

On 29 May 1952, three hundred seventy-seven questionnaires were sent to major superiors of women's communities. The questions touched on areas of basic statistical information, the training program of the religious community, and the present practice of sister-lay teacher ratio. "It [the Survey] was a hard-hitting thing. We wanted direct answers. We sent it out to all the active Orders and the amazing thing is the high percentage of responses, 80% was an unheard of response to a questionnaire. . . .The most amazing thing is--they were told just in passing, 'If you have other comments you wish to make, use the reverse of the sheet'--I can't tell you how many sheets we had; those poor superiors just poured out their hearts, they were so delighted that somebody was going to do something."[20]

The first summary of two hundred fifty-five responses was tabulated in the report which was distributed to the Major Superiors of Women before the August 1952 Notre Dame Conference. Those responding represented eighty-one percent of all teaching Sisters in the United States and represented communities active in all parts of America. The survey results contained comments and statements of the mother superiors on the education of sisters, vocations, extra-scholastic burdens upon sister-teachers, lay teachers, and financial problems.

By October 1952, a revised edition of the survey report was made available to the Bishops' Committee on Education through the NCEA. This revision contained a financial report gathered from surveying a smaller group of religious communities. Twenty-five communities representing 23,000 sisters had been chosen for this part of the study. The percentage of income-producing members in each community, the annual cost of living, and the salaries of the sisters were some of the areas covered in the questionnaire. It was determined that in forty-five percent of the communities studied, the average annual cost of living per sister exceeded the average annual salary of the sister; that according to calculations it would take the average sister thirty years of teaching to pay back to her community the monetary cost of one year of college, leaving no funds for retirement. In November 1952, Msgr. F. N. Pitt, chairman of the Teacher Education Section, presented the findings and recommendations of the Survey to the annual meeting of Diocesan Superintendents. "It was the first time I heard public tribute and credit given to religious communities, not only for our Catholic school system but also for educating teachers for a hundred years without cost to a diocese or parish,"[21] wrote Brother William Mang, CSC.

The scene painted by the survey results was not a happy one. It confirmed the fact that little was being done to improve sister-education. Statistics showed that fifty-eight communities were sending out sisters with less than thirty hours of college credit and one hundred-eighteen communities had neither educational facilities of their own nor easy access to another Catholic college or university. Thirty-three states already demanded a degree to teach and only thirteen communities had a degree program in operation for their sisters. All this pointed to some discouraging circumstances. In addition there was the recognition that there were sisters already in teaching relegated to spending the next ten to twenty summers working to get their degree. Militating against any improvement were always the great demand for sisters and the lack of an immediate supply necessary to fit the need. Lay teachers were needed. However, the survey on teacher-preparation revealed that:

The respondents point out quite frankly that lay teachers are unacceptable to many pastors--mainly because of the higher salary required. It is the consensus of opinion that the acceptance of lay teachers will come about only if there is action on a national scale, and that such action could best and most effectively be initiated and directed by ecclesiastical authority.[22]

The Survey Committee after studying the results of both questionnaires, recommended a three-point program to be presented to ecclesiastical and educational authorities. The recommendations were given according to the stated needs of the surveyed communities.

1. The national establishment of a 20% or 4-and-1 lay teacher ratio, with the burden of this arrangement averaged in a diocese, so as to fall upon parishes in proportion to their financial ability to assume it.

2. A general readjustment of salary scales for religious teachers, with stipends so arranged on a twelve-month basis as to make more adequate provision for today's cost of living, for the community care of the infirm and retired, and above all for the proper professional preparation of the Sisters.

3. A statement by the Hierarchy applying to local conditions or defining for the American scene of action the recent directives from the Holy Father and from the Sacred Congregation regarding the training of religious--both as to its quantitative aspect by comparison with secular teachers, and as to its specific quality as for teachers who are at once themselves religious and quasi-official participants in the magisterium of the Church.[23]

A brief run-down of the high points in the study indicates the reasons behind the recommendations. Only thirty-seven of the two hundred fifty-five communities responding to the survey gave their sisters four or more years of training. In the 1952-53 school year, 5,409 sisters were requested for replacements or expansion in schools with only 2,058 sisters ready for those positions. During the previous five years, two hundred-five communities had received a total of 4,227 requests from pastors to open new schools, requests that they could not fill.

. . . what many of the laity never realized was the fact that the sisters' salaries (which at this time were about $30 a month) was expected to cover food, clothing, health, education and other ordinary expenses, telephone, laundry, cleaning supplies, etc. In addition, provisions had to be made for the aged and chronically ill sisters of the community. Most parishioners thought that in addition to the housing provided by the parish, all other living expenses were also provided for the sisters as they were for the priests living in the rectories. This was not the case.[24]

To summarize the situation: sisters were eager to do everything in their power to solve the problems made by the greatly expanding school population. However, any solution to the combination of directives and difficulties which confronted them went quite beyond their unassisted resources. On the one hand, there were the repeated exhortations of the Holy Father and the religious congresses to improve the quality of religious formation, the sharply upgraded state requirements for certification, and the increased expectations of parents with regard to the general and specialized background of their children's teachers. On the other hand, there was the sister-shortage and the drain that had been made on community finances by inflation and added educational costs. It was becoming obvious that any action would have to be radical and corporate. No religious community could do it alone.

The Survey Committee felt, therefore, that the various contacts it had made with communities authorized it to suggest that the three-point program was a fair representation of the minds of women religious as to the assistance they hoped to get from the ecclesiastical and educational authorities for whom the investigation had been undertaken. The responses of the major superiors indicated a feeling of impatience to move ahead. "The thinking aroused, the sharing of common problems, and the possibility of some unified action, gave the Sisters new hope and broadened horizons."[25]

The response of the hierarchy to the survey varied. Cardinal Samuel Stritch, Archdiocese of Chicago, wrote:

> I thank you very much for sending me a copy of your committee's survey on the problem of teacher training for our schools. I hope that you will continue this study. The statistics which you present are very interesting and do represent a great problem. I think that if we had more thinking on this subject, we would be able to work out a plan and program. The large communities, of course, can work out a very reasonable program with the facilities which they have and the facilities which are available to them. My concern

is for the small communities. I think that more study will bring a solution of this whole problem. Once we have a real program, we shall be able to educate others so as to put it into effect.[26]

Bishop Fulton J. Sheen after reading the report advocated the working out of a special curriculum just for sisters. But all in all, there was no impetus for action from the bishops' group. Somehow they did not sense the extent of the problem or the need for immediacy in addressing it. Msgr. Pitt, however, sensed both. He supported the project and offered valuable statistics. In 1941-42, lay teachers made up thirteen percent of the total number of teachers in Catholic schools while in 1950-51, they made up only eleven percent. The number of religious teachers increased from 76,861 to 94,078 between 1940 and 1950. Even though that was an increase of twenty-two percent, the increase was not sufficient to match the increased enrollment of thirty-four percent in the elementary schools and forty-two percent in the secondary schools. Msgr. Pitt wrote:

> Hence, even though there are more religious teachers today there is definitely, as your study shows, a need for more vocations and a need for a greater number of lay teachers to teach in our schools. Since I have been in school work I know of no activity which is more needed than the one undertaken by your committee. Nor has there been any project which has aroused more discussion among Catholic educators as the facts are spread around more broadly. The interest, as well as the discussion, is growing.[27]

Soon Msgr. Pitt again indicated how necessary he felt it was to disseminate the information of the survey.

> The whole question of your valuable report; that is, of the teacher situation in general, assumes more importance daily. We hope that the program outlined for our Atlantic City meeting will clarify a number of questions on which there is some disagreement. It is rather paradoxical to realize at this late date in the history of Catholic education that the sisters who alone have made the Catholic elementary school system possible still have a selling job to do with so many of our Catholic leaders and educators. One thing you have already done and this is: you have aroused their interest by your report. However, I am still convinced that too few of our leaders actually realize the seriousness of the situation.[28]

The sisters of the committee had tried and kept trying to make the findings of the survey known to the right people. Mother Mary Florence, SL, was added to the committee in September 1952. It was becoming evident as comments came in from the privately circulated survey report that the problems raised were perhaps too great for the annual session of the Teacher Education Section of the NCEA. Much time before the 1953 NCEA Convention was spent in letter writing. The committee was hindered both by non-receptiveness from some and by the constraint that they could not make all the facts public as confidentiality had been pledged to all filling out the survey. Sister Mary Emil also reported that a common fear of the day, Communism, also had an influence on how the survey results would be reported: "The Communists would have a fine time with these figures."[29] The privacy that had surrounded religious life for so long was being guarded. All of this explains the fact that the gathered information was largely left unanalyzed.

It was not until mid 1953, however, and after the 1953 NCEA convention, that copies of the survey were sent to all diocesan superintendents. Frustration can be sensed in this comment of Msgr. McManus, Assistant Director of the Department of Education of the NCWC:

> Your latest report on Cost of Living and Education certainly presents impressive evidence of an urgent need to raise the salaries of teaching Sisters. I am still struggling with the problem of the best way to persuade the members of the Hierarchy to face the facts about the teacher shortage and the serious financial plight of most religious communities.[30]

A copy of the survey results made its way in an unofficial manner to Archbishop Paul Philippe, OP, in Rome. It was Archbishop Philippe who suggested that copies be sent to Cardinal Pizzardo, Prefect of the Congregation of the Universities, and to Cardinal Valeri, Prefect of the Congregation of Religious. The response of Sister Mary Richardine Quirk, BVM, indicates the cautious action of the survey committee:

> I did not feel free to do so since our committee was not authorized to communicate directly with the hierarchy but only with religious--the channeling of the Survey information to the hierarchy has been through the groups set up for that purpose in this country, that is the NCEA and the NCWC Department of Education. I took the liberty to send confidential copies of our material to you because of your close association with the religious of the United States.[31]

Early in 1953, the Survey Committee busied itself with one practical task to meet at least one of the needs indicated by the survey results. This task--the compilation of a list of religious communities having four-year colleges and willing to open their institutions to members of other religious communities on a cost basis only--was a monumental undertaking. *The Directory of Catholic Women's Colleges* was published twice and was a valuable resource for communities looking for educational possibilities for their sisters both on the undergraduate and graduate level.

Sister Education and the Professional Standards Commission

The need for an organizational arrangement for sisters that would allow for the exchange of ideas and the planning of new programs was becoming clearer to the Survey Committee. To draw together higher superiors, college personnel and those engaged in formation was seen as the next step. It was at the 1953 NCEA convention that another public step toward such a formal organization for sister education took place. In one year, the sisters had organized a committee of key sister leaders, administered a questionnaire that revealed some glaring needs in sisters' education, and had tried with some level of success to disseminate the results. For the 1953 NCEA convention, the sisters were again summoned to give a "part" of a presentation and once again it was through the Teacher Education Section.

The purpose of the joint meeting of the Teacher Education Section and the Superintendents' Section was explained thus by Msgr. Pitt:

> It seems to me that the primary purpose of our joint meeting is to call to the attention of all Catholic educators the extremely grave problem that is confronting all of our schools, particularly the elementary schools today and tomorrow. The problem is what can we do to provide sufficient teachers to meet the ever growing mass of children crowding into our schools. Your survey and report have pin-pointed this problem. If we can emphasize the seriousness of the situation we are hopeful that some useful suggestions will come from its discussion.[32]

The sisters of the survey committee had hoped that they would be given at least a half-day in which to explain, discuss, and plan. Instead, however, the sisters were told they would have fifteen minutes in which to tell their story. This time constraint was an example of the dependence experienced by these women religious. The time limit could be interpreted as de-emphasizing the importance of sister education, an interpretation substantiated by a lack of support from some school superintendents.   Disappointed but undaunted, the sisters adapted a different strategy.

With determined planning, the sisters decided that the fifteen minute time span was to be used not to speak about the survey but rather to voice the need for sisters to have their own planning organization within the NCEA. The Survey Committee felt bolstered to stand in front of the group with this request because they had tried it out on those attending the March 1953 Midwest regional meeting of the NCEA and had been unanimously approved. There the Survey Committee had presented a proposal, based on the results of the survey, that an organization be set up, within the NCEA, and limited to sisters only. This organization would be devoted to the educational problems of sisters. The Midwest group, comprised chiefly of college administrators and professors, felt it was a worthwhile proposal and gave it a vote of confidence. They felt that if seminaries and superintendents could have their organization, then the sisters could too.

At the NCEA, Msgr. Carl J. Ryan, representing the superintendents, spoke first and gave a sympathetic review of the findings of the survey. He was supportive of the needs of the sisters and he stressed the need for religious communities to communicate their financial needs to diocesan authorities.

> Practically everyone realizes that sisters' salaries are too low. On the other hand, it is a very common belief that sisters have other sources of income such as gifts, music lessons, bookstore proceeds, etc. I suppose that in most cases, even where there is this extra income, it still falls short of the actual needs per sister.[33]

Msgr. Ryan went on to note the need of lay teachers in the system. His suggestion, however, of educating sisters with the lay teachers would become something of a bone of contention all through the early years of the Sister Formation Conference. Msgr. Ryan doubted the possibility of setting a national norm of one lay teacher to every four sisters. He suggested, rather, that this situation be left to the discretion of each diocese. Ryan recognized the need for a college education for sisters but was willing to allow communities, particularly those that were giving less than two years of preparation to their sisters, the time to build this up to four years.

In her short presentation, Sister Mary Emil commented on Msgr. Ryan's talk and pleaded for a separate sister organization. Her statement concerning the financial plight of sisters explained an attitude, almost a condition of sisters at the time. "Sisters are afraid. They do not wish to be mercenary. They are trained to endure. They have been too timid to act in isolation and they have no institutionalized manner of acting together."[34]

Her strong plea for an organization for sisters and by sisters was eloquent:

> . . . and I am submitting that the teaching Sisters of the country
> need an organization of their own, in which to formulate, and by
> which to present, their considered and united requests and
> proposals. . . .The success of TEPS [Teacher Education and
> Professional Standards] has been due to organization. We feel that
> we need to match that organization. Their success is further
> attributed to the spread of the idea that the teacher, the
> practitioner, is responsible for the standards of her profession. I
> venture to say that we will see improvement in pre-service
> training, in-service training, salary schedules and all similar lines
> for Sisters, when we put over the idea that the Sister is responsible
> for the standards in her vocation. . . . It may be in place here to
> point out that inasmuch as the proposed group would be a
> Sister-Education and Professional Standards Commission [SEPS],
> it should be understood from the beginning that it would be an
> organization of Sisters and for Sisters.[35]

Sister Mary Emil pleaded not only for a separate organization but that this group within the NCEA would issue a strong statement that nothing less than a four-year degree would be acceptable preparation for a sister teacher. She went one step further by asking that the degree be based on theology and philosophy. The education for sisters was to be different than that for a lay teacher. Sister Mary Emil herself related in a talk given in later years to her own sisters:

> So we went to Atlantic City and used up our precious 15 minutes
> making a plea for an organization of our own--so that the Sisters
> could meet in the different areas, exchange ideas and facilities,
> work out common projects, and so on. We pointed out that we
> would always use the men in a consultative capacity, but that we
> needed some opportunity to talk quietly and prudently among
> ourselves in a situation where the enthusiasm and dynamism of
> some could be tempered by the prudence and wisdom of others.
> It was a reasonable proposal, and hard to find reasons against it.
> After quite a lengthy discussion in which some of the
> Superintendents used all their ammunition, the group voted
> unanimously to accept the proposal, subject to the provision that
> it would have to be approved by the Executive Committee of the
> Department, and the GenralExecutive [sic] Board of the
> Association.[36]

It was Msgr. Pitt who made that proposal:

> That the present Survey Committee on Teacher Preparation be
> enlarged by the addition of a representative from all interested
> communities and that it be empowered as an integrating group in
> order to sponsor exploratory regional conferences at interested
> institutions, with a view to the ultimate establishment of Sisters
> Educational and Professional Standards Commissions.[37]

Now the waiting began. It would take another full year before complete
approval of this proposal would come through. Sister Mary Emil, as chairperson
of the still existing Survey Committee, felt it necessary to ask that the following
projects go on in the interim: study of the status of sister-education and of the
problems faced by religious communities; study of the educational standing of the
country's sister-teachers; continuation of the financial study and an interpretation
of the results in the light of the effects of inflation on the cost of living;
publication of the College Directory in an annual edition which included a list of
available scholarships. This list of projects would become the work agenda for
the Sister Formation Conference once it became approved. Always trying to
place the needs of the sisters in a realistic context, Sister Mary Emil stated:

> Now important as all this data is I feel that it is not as significant
> for the plans we must make for the future as first--what is going
> on in the public schools, and secondly, what is the trend in teacher
> education generally. The situation in the public schools to which
> I refer may be summed up under four heads--shortages, crowding,
> low salaries and poor teachers.[38]

Sister Mary Emil had looked into the teacher shortage and come up with two
reasons for it: the war and an increasing population.

The war drew thirty-three percent of the teachers away from their profession
for higher paying jobs. This loss came when the population began to increase,
an increase that was estimated to continue until 1960. The condition of
overcrowding that the NEA was asking all parents to investigate in the public
schools was designated as any regular class over thirty and any language or
special class over twenty-five. The average teacher salary in 1952 was $3360
with the average of all employed persons at $3390 and those of the professions
at $9120. "It was stated in our Congress last year by Senator Fulbright that in
Detroit beginning teachers get a lower initial salary than prison cooks, comfort
station attendants, dogcatchers, animal keepers at the zoo, garbage collector
foreman, rat exterminator."[39]

All these facts were significant. Thinking about sisters' standards against this backdrop put some perspective into anticipated action. Understanding that the Catholic schools did not operate in a vacuum but were a part of the whole educational system was a first step. As the public sector began arousing opinion about the dramatically poor status of education, the Catholic system also had to work on the problems of inferior teacher-preparation, overcrowding, and inadequate remuneration.

> It would seem then that it is our job to sell our Catholic public--all the way from superintendents, to pastors, to people--the idea that we are going into a period where the Catholic schools, like the public schools, will need more support--that the Sisters have tried to make up for all the shortages and to ease all the stresses and strains almost alone, but that as much as we would wish to spend ourselves to the last drop of sweat and ounce of blood, there is a limit to how far we will stretch, and that for the good of all Catholic education we will have to rethink what we are willing to pay for it.[40]

Looking to the public sector as a norm, Sister Mary Emil suggested that just as the National Commission on Teacher Education and Professional Standards adopted a resolution on 18 February 1952, that salaries be high enough to justify the four years of education needed above high school and the fifth year before acceptance to full professional status, so this same norm should be adopted for sister teachers. The trend in colleges toward the need of a liberal arts or general education was also to be considered. This trend was affecting teacher education at Harvard, Cornell, and the University of Louisville where experimental programs were being run with assistance from the Ford Foundation. These programs spread the professional training of teachers to the fifth and in some cases even the sixth year of college because students had to first complete a broad four-year liberal arts program.

Much frustration can be sensed in Sister Mary Emil's statement to college and university administrators:

> Last year in Atlantic City I was a member of a panel which was asked to discuss the following question--I quote--"Shall we lower our standards to meet the present circumstances? If so, how much?" For the past two years at the N.C.E.A. Conventions there have been proposed "emergency two year programs" for the training of Sisters. Your own president, Father Murphy, whose sympathies, I know, are with the Sisters and their problems,

thought it well to suggest to me that I should discuss today "whether we can go along with the two year minimum college training for the time, or whether we must be intractable and hold for a four-year minimum." I agree with him completely that this question must still be discussed, but I submit as my personal opinion that it is one of the most tragic aspects of the American educational scene that while the public school people are asking "How can we raise standards?" the Catholics should be asking "Can we hold our standards or shall we lower them?"[41]

College and university administrators clearly recognized that improved sister education could add to both the spiritual and mental health and the professional stability of the sisters as well as enhance their contribution to the Church. These educational leaders valued intellectualism and wanted to see it fostered in sister-educators. Along with the core leaders of sister formation, they agreed with the NEA Platform which stated: "Their [teachers'] preparation should provide rich cultural background, adequate professional training, thorough knowledge of subjectmatter [sic] . . . a well-developed social consciousness . . . a professional attitude in regard to self-improvement."[42]

Sister Mary Emil summed up the situation at hand in her own incisive manner and challenged:

Are our Sisters intellectual? The vast majority of them have been educated, if they have earned degrees at all, on the twenty-year plan--that is by an agglomeration of summer school credits for courses pursued in various institutions and in peculiar sequences. Those who hold B.A.'s of that kind will be the first to tell you that they do not really have college educations. If a Sister spends the years almost up to her silver jubilee painfully acquiring the training with which she should have begun, if she is conscious of her inadequacies during all that time and long after, if she is expected to mix with her teaching and class preparation a generous portion of cleaning, sewing, cooking and even janitor work, and If [sic] all of this must be crammed into the intervals between her spiritual and community exercises, is there any wonder that her love of learning is somewhat dimmed, and that she does not inspire scholarly enthusiasm in her pupils? Now there are many potential college teachers and many potential "distinguished scholars" in the Sisterhoods. Many of those Sisters are now teaching in the elementary school and will probably stay there--for a kind of accidental reason. By the time their undergraduate record has accumulated to indicate their power, they are almost too old to warrant the investment of Ph.D. Training.[43]

The task was great and would demand that adequate pre-service and in-service training for sisters be provided along with the consideration of new methods, procedures, and curriculum planning. Key to this planning was the firm conviction of many sisters that an education for a sister was to be different--better--than that of her lay counterparts; thus the serious consideration of what the ratio studiorum for a teaching sister should be. "Does the Sister's need of an intellectual grasp of the principles of the spiritual life, does her status as religion teacher and moral counsellor, and her quasi-official role in the Church indicate a need for differently organized basic training?"[44] The issues of intellectualism and the belief that sisters were different from the laity would both be topics of heated debate among sisters and others as the definition of sister formation came to be discussed. Wrote Sister Mary Richardine:

> I do not believe it is cynicism, but a bare statement of fact, to say that the Sisters are considered only in so far as they can meet the need in the schools. Their needs as human beings, consecrated and dedicated to the service of God, seem to be completely ignored. Their limitations, in having almost super-human burdens placed upon them, seem also to be ignored. Their rights, even though as individuals they may not consider them, cannot be overlooked by those responsible to God for the training of the God-given talents which these Sisters possess.[45]

A juncture in the road had come for sister teachers and for all American women religious; dependence was giving way to independence, as sisters, compelled to speak what was just and necessary, were being heard on issues that touched their very style of life. And even though it may have seemed that only those attending the NCEA were listening, the structures that would open up to sisters or crumble to allow them room to grow would prove that others were becoming aware of the educational and financial needs of American women religious.

The Survey Committee was still hard at work. The Committee waited from April 1953 when they were given hope that a sisters' organization would be possible, until January 1954 when final approval for the Sister Formation Conference was given by the General Executive Board of the NCEA. During this time there was a planning meeting for the 1954 NCEA convention that showed the issue of sister education was alive but not yet settled.

The Board discussed at some length a proposal from the Section on Teacher Education with the College and University Department to set up a series of SEPS, commissions on Sister Education and Professional Standards. The matter was referred to the Executive Committee of the College and University Department for discussion at its fall meeting with the understanding that it would be discussed again by the Executive Board in light of the reaction of the Department Executive Committee. Meantime, the proposal can be receiving further consideration and study by all concerned.[46]

The Executive Committee asked Sister Mary Emil to attend its October meeting. All forty-two participants had been sent a copy of the survey and a personal letter. The committee asked Sister Mary Emil many questions about SEPS and were satisfied with her answers. They passed a resolution to support the proposal. Sister Mary Emil was also commissioned by Father Meyer, head of the College and University Department, to read a paper on sister education at the department's plenary session at the 1954 NCEA convention. The constant support of the department evidenced their early understanding of the significance of sister education.

A supportive visit from Mother Teresa, IHM, Sister Mary Emil's superior, to Msgr. Hochwalt on 15 March 1954 was pivotal in accomplishing the establishment of the Sister Formation Conference. Msgr. Hochwalt gave permission to the sister group to hold regional conferences (one in each NCEA region yearly), to hold a closed meeting of mothers general, heads of religious communities, or their representatives at the 1954 NCEA Convention, and to set up as a formal section in the NCEA. This set of permissions by the executive secretary of the NCEA put everything into order and the convention of 1954 made the Sister Formation Conference official.

Sister Formation Conference

Chicago, the convention site of the NCEA in 1954, became the official birthplace of the Sister Formation Conference, when after six years of NCEA conventions, this one would give sisters their own organization. During Monday's meeting of the Executive Committee the decision was made to study until Thursday the proposal for a sisters' section. On Tuesday, the College and University Department met. On Wednesday of the NCEA convention, the first meeting of the major superiors was held. Msgr. Hochwalt arranged to have a private dining room available at the Conrad Hilton Hotel for the closed meeting of the designated representatives of the major superiors. A card was needed for admittance to this meeting.

The purpose of the Wednesday meeting was to plan, and a great deal of planning led by Sister Mary Emil and her committee took place in a short time. The operating structure of the SFC was decided. It was recommended by the group that the survey committee take the leadership role of the new group in conjunction with a national consultative committee made up of superintendents. Sister Formation Regional Conferences would be established to conform to the six NCEA regions. Each region would have a planning committee that would work with a survey committee member to adapt the national theme to the special needs of the area. This committee was made up of a superintendent of schools, dean of advanced studies of a member college or university, religious prefect of studies, a religious canon lawyer, two officers of the NCEA regional unit of the college and university department, and a free choice of the region. Further it was determined that two-day institutes be held in every region to begin to discuss major issues of concern. Even the idea of the Sister Formation Bulletin, an internal organ of communication, was introduced at this meeting.

For this new organization, the name Sister Formation Conference was accepted rather than Sisters Educational and Professional Standards Commission. This name change signified a growth in thinking. Not wishing to serve strictly the professional needs of the sister, this conference desired to extend its scope to "Sister-formation in all its aspects--spiritual, intellectual, and professional training and their fitting integration in pre-service and in-service programs."[47] This enlarged the concept of teacher preparation from that of specific points of professional education to that of a general concept of total education. With these plans voiced, the Executive Committee of the NCEA said yes to the legal status of the Sister Formation Committee and placed it under the college and university department, the very department that first fostered interest in sister education. At this same NCEA convention, the Teacher Education Section expanded its focus to include lay teachers. Started as a special group in the NCEA to study the problems of improving standards in sister-education, this group would now devote its energies to the education of all involved in the Catholic system.

As sisters, superintendents, and others left the 1954 convention, there must have been mixed feelings of anticipation, exhilaration, and cautious wondering. A large group of active, energetic, and intelligent women had been given the approval to form their own group. The talk that Sister Mary Emil was invited to give at this convention penetratingly summed up the concerns of the day and of the sisters and once again pointed dramatically to what needed to be done:

> American Sisters are wonderful, obedient, devoted, self-sacrificing
> and resourceful women . . . [yet] the present system of Sister-

training militates against the discovery and development of talent in the Sisterhoods. Because of the pressure from the parishes for more and more Sisters, and because of the failure thus far to introduce lay teachers on the lower levels in sufficient numbers to release Sisters for necessary education, there is never time to educate anyone for a future need. The talented Sisters, like the others, get the degrees by the summer-school plan. By the time they are ready for graduate training, and by the time they have proven special fitness for it, they are almost too old to make it economical . . . we have never looked upon our Sisters as a human resource to be used to the utmost intellectual capacity of each one--perhaps because they are women, perhaps because things go slowly in the Church and teaching nuns are still a novelty, and perhaps because we have so many of them. Which all is a little like saying that we have been thinking that Sisters are expendable . . .[48]

Conclusion

With the forming of the Sister Formation Conference, a vehicle for institutional change was put into action. Now the voices of some far-seeing American women religious would be heard as they directed this organization toward planned change. Representing the grassroots, these charismatic women formed their own elite group possessing a vision others did not always share.

Charismatic leadership would allow for the goals of sister formation to be accomplished. Sister Mary Emil, the chairperson of the Survey Committee and eventually the first national executive secretary of the SFC possessed the talents needed. Those who joined her shared like qualities and their efforts were rewarded as growth occurred from within and without. Two key steps were taken: membership in the SFC was made positional, not personal, and the SFC regions were determined by those already existing for the NCEA. Invitations to all meetings were sent to apostolic communities and were intended for the major superior of the community, the directress of formation, and the directress of studies. If a community owned and operated a college, the president or dean was also invited. Depending on the topic to be discussed, the postulant, novitiate, or juniorate directress received the formation invitation. All this allowed for a sharing among all who had an important role in the formation of the sister. Each region, given the ability to be autonomous while observing the general by-laws of the SFC, dealt with problems specific to its area. Early on this demonstrated to all sisters that sister formation principles were not to be imposed on any community from without but rather came from a joint recognition of need.

Convincing the major superiors of the need for a reformed formation was key to the success of the newly founded SFC and the topics of the first regional conferences would help to educate communities from the inside out. Having to cut through long community traditions of education was another challenge. These sister leaders would have to be convincing as to why the younger generation needed an education previous sisters were never given. "The senior sisters were concerned that younger sisters were now able to get an education, an education that these sisters had to work all their lives for."[49]

Sister Ritamary Bradley, CHM, the first editor of the Sister Formation Bulletin, summed up this era by stating:

> All of this was very new to everybody and anyone in authority was uneasy because sisters had really never taken leadership, they had never been organized and there was a great deal of uneasiness. But there was also a great deal of vision, there were a lot of people in the hierarchy and persons in different communities who began to see where this was leading. But they thought it was a threat to obedience, to humility, a threat to religious life in general.[50]

Convinced that the formation of the religious should include the intellectual, social, and psychological aspects of the person along with the spiritual, the leadership sought a process that would form effective and healthy ministers. Orchestration of the critical shifts in religious life was taking place and women were gradually recognizing the need to direct their own destiny. The conference was sanctioned and a road map approved for new plans. The needs of sisters were being recognized by sisters themselves and were becoming known to others. Now, in order to meet those needs, more work would have to be done, and sisters would indeed have to struggle together to meet the challenge of what it meant to adequately and professionally serve the Church in the modern world. "Sister Lucy" was on her way to being educated in a fuller manner.

CHAPTER II   OPERATION BOOTSTRAP 1954-1957

The idea of studying and having a degree before stepping into the elementary and high school classroom was counter to the traditional way of educating sisters. Previously only practical training and professional teaching courses had readied most sisters for the classroom. This initial preparation had been supplemented with the twenty-year summer school plan that would eventually end with the acquisition of a degree. This method did not demand travel, great expense, or time away from the convent atmosphere. To acquire a degree before going into the classroom meant a turnabout in thinking and a renovation of the educational plan. When religious superiors, formation directresses, and directresses of studies were faced with the challenge to update, it was with the Church's blessing that sisters acted. The needs of the Church and of their sisters were the impetus to forge ahead.

Insufficient future planning, low salaries, and the inability of communities to make decisions on their own were conditions necessitating changes in religious life at this time. The poor educational standards among sisters placed religious communities in a critical situation and only by working together could communities begin to change their situation. Also, the Congregation of Religious had encouraged religious communities around the world to begin working with one another in connection with the recommended religious reforms of Pius XII. The Sister Formation Conference (SFC) was the first organization in America to facilitate this type of sharing. Only in 1956 would a formal organization representing women's communities, the Conference of Major Women's Superiors be founded. So the years 1954-1957 saw the beginning of active cooperation between and within religious communities. With a reason to come together, religious communities began to plan and share with one another, thus creating a united front.

One distinctive shift was that sisters were beginning to state their needs, a thing unheard of in the past. As sisters began to speak, they did so within an organization approved by the Church. The Sister Formation Conference within the NCEA became the official mouthpiece of sisters and the *Sister Formation Bulletin* became a written record of all that was happening. Communities of American women religious began to assert the position that self-direction was as possible now as it had been in the early history of each community and that such direction was not contrary to religious life.

An imperceptible shift was also taking place within religious life. It was a shift that began to allow for the recognition of the uniqueness of each sister. Colorful and individual personalities emerged in leadership roles of the SFC. Approved by the major superiors but not major superiors themselves, these women possessed high degrees of education and were determined to make it possible for all women religious to have equal educational opportunities. The energy of the SFC was generated by consideration of the total formation of the young woman as a human being, a Christian, and a religious. From this formation, the personal identity of the woman religious was expected to emerge.

In the field of education, the shifts of this time were the easiest to perceive. The NCEA in conjunction with and patterning itself after the action of the National Education Association (NEA) sought to require, implement, and protect adequate training for the religious sisters and the lay teacher. Growing concerns included the reputation of Catholic education, the increasing presence of lay teachers and the high percentage of Catholic students not in Catholic schools. It was through the NCEA that the hierarchy, school superintendents, and religious and state officials were urged to cooperate in beginning a systematic plan for teacher training to change the educational status of sisters. This cooperation was not always easily achieved as in the particular case where an American bishop believed that the NCEA had subversive connections with the NEA.

"Operation Bootstrap," a phrase coined by Sister Mary Emil to summarize the early years of the SFC, was an appropriate description of the work of these years. Through "Operation Bootstrap" sisters were to pull themselves up by their own energies to an adequate professional level. From there they could go one step higher to a professional competency that would allow for a trained leadership in the Church. Raising sisters to this next step came to be known as "Operation Airlift." During the years 1954-1957, the SFC had the status of a temporary committee in the college and university department of the NCEA. At this time, the SFC clarified its purpose and worked out its organizational structure. The first authorization for this committee was given for five years.

General Schema

The leadership fell to Sister Mary Emil Penet, IHM, the original chairperson of the Survey Committee, by the appointment of Brother Bonaventure Thomas, FSC, president of the college and university department. From the beginning,

Sister was able to articulate the needs of sisters, make these needs known, and go forward.

Into the promotion of Sister Formation, Sister Mary Emil poured all her rare talents: a keen and disciplined intellect, a grasp of psychological factors, a sense of timing, convincing speech, organizational ability and--unlimited devotion. In the interests of Sister Formation, she traveled thousand of miles, speaking sometimes to hundreds of sisters in metropolitan areas; again, to select groups of community personnel; and, very frequently, to Mothers Superior of small, isolated communities, to whom she brought light, encouragement, and suggested solutions for their educational problems. Through her untiring efforts, Sister Formation came to be known, understood and desired.[1]

Joining Sister Mary Emil were former members of the Survey Committee, Sister Mary Basil, SSND; Sister Celine, CR; Mother Mary Florence, SL; Sister Gerard, OSF; Sister Mary Richardine Quirk, BVM and one additional member, Sister M. Emmanuel Collins, OSF. This committee would now be known as the National Sister Formation Committee. Later, as the growth and development of the SFC continued, the committee was broadened to include Mother Ann Dengel, SCMM, superior general and foundress of the Medical Missionary Sisters, who represented the nursing sisters, and Sister Frederica Horvath, SSS, superior general of the Sisters of Social Service, who represented the sisters in social work.

Systematic building took place to help sisters. A highly structured process was followed to organize "Operation Bootstrap" and evidenced the foresight present in the leadership of Sister Mary Emil and her committee. Specific areas were designated for action. Adequate professional pre-service training for all sister teachers, nurses, and social workers was advocated. According to the Church, a juniorate segment that would supplement novitiate training was to be planned. The juniorate was to be an exclusive time for spiritual and professional formation for a period of not less than two years after the novitiate and under the direction of a trained directress. Spiritual and intellectual enrichment as part of the pre-service college program was already seen as a possible topic for discussion. The needs of the sister already in service became a research topic. Lastly, on-going formation that would allow sisters to keep up with current events, thought, and culture was considered a priority. Constantly aware of the power of an organized group with a vision, the leadership of the SFC sought to sharpen the power and force of American women religious. "At that point we may begin to think of what an influence 154,000 Sisters could be in the spiritual, intellectual, and apostolic life of the Church and of our nation."[2]

With the juniorate movement clearly mandated at the 1952 Roman Congress for General Superiors of Women's Institutes, mothers general knew that something had to be done to comply. It was, however, the belief of the SFC that guaranteeing that every sister would have a bachelor's degree was not enough. The education sought was the development of the total person. This sister-formation was to be defined as an integration of the spiritual and intellectual training necessary for the needs of the times and on a level that at least matched secular teachers in terms of American standards.

The Organization of the Sister Formation Conference

The organization of the Sister Formation Conference as a temporary committee within the college and university department of the NCEA was directed by two committees: National Sister Formation Committee as described earlier (sister consultants) and the National Consultative Committee (priest consultants).[3] The latter Consultative Committee consisted of a superintendent of schools, a dean of studies, a religious prefect of studies, a religious canon lawyer, two officers of the regional unit of the University and College Department, a Survey Committee member and a member at large. The priests chosen to be the first National Consultative Committee, a liaison and advising group with a three-year term of membership, were Father Bryan J. McEntegart, Msgr. Frederick G. Hochwalt, Msgr. John J. Voight, Father Paul C. Reinert, SJ, Father Allan P. Farrell, SJ, Father Cyril F. Meyer, CM, and Father John F. Murphy. Certain expectations were placed on this consulting committee as noted by Sr. Mary Emil:

> I am quite conscious that we have had the temerity to ask some of the businest [sic] and most responsible persons in Catholic education to serve on the National Consultative Committee. In doing so, I promised in each case, that the work would not be burdensome. . . .I hope not to have to trouble you with the kind of organizational detail that the Sisters can handle by themselves. It seems to me now, however, that there are three areas in which we shall need assistance: 1) public relations, 2) content of our programs, 3) finances. . . .The work we have begun holds prospect of good for the Sisterhoods whose full extent is hard to imagine at this point. I know that I can count not only on your advice but on your prayers.[4]

The first assignment given to these men was to respond to the following questions: 1) what major problems in sister education should we be addressing? 2) what advice would you give on the time and manner of asking the local bishops for their blessings on the Conference? 3) what comments, advice or questions would you offer?

The role of this committee can not be underrated. The presence of their names on the official stationery of the SFC was coveted. Often one of these men opened a door that would otherwise have been closed to sisters, a significant point that demonstrated not just the power of men in the church, but the need of the SFC to engage male support of this movement. On the educational scene, these men knew situations first-hand and could verify that the work of the SFC was needed.

Meetings of the National Sister Formation Conference were held annually at the NCEA convention while the regional meetings were held yearly in each geographic region. Admission to both national and regional meetings was determined by invitation and by community position; higher superiors, novice and juniorate mistresses, and educational advisers were the usual delegates. From the beginning, these positions were determined as key to community change and renovation. Intrinsic to and necessary for integrated sister formation was the coordination of each community's work of leadership along with spiritual and educational formation. The regional conferences especially allowed for a kind of cross-pollination of ideas, philosophy and purposes. According to Sister Bertrande Meyers, mutual help and sharing were built into the structure of the meetings:

> When one keeps in mind that the delegates all occupied key positions in their respective Communities, positions that made for great influence, one grasps the far-reaching benefits derived from these regional meetings. Representatives from large, medium-sized and small Communities met; useful information was shared and offers of services exchanged. Mutual help kindled growing hope, and Sister Formation became more and more a household word.[5]

1954-55 SFC Regional Conferences and NCEA Conventions

The regional conferences were to allow for an exchange of ideas and to provide mutual support for communities. To organize the first regional meetings, the National Sister Formation Committee met with regional chairpersons after having a plan of action approved by the National Consultative Committee. The first of these planning sessions took place in May, 1954. Aware that some communities may not have been present at the previous NCEA convention, a general letter was composed and sent to all religious communities from the appropriate regional chairperson. This letter explained how the SFC had come about and invited all communities to participate in the Conference. It was a goal of the SFC to involve as many communities as possible. Later when Sister Mary Emil and others began to visit and consult with individual communities, no community, whatever its needs, was excluded.

The theme of the first year's conferences was carefully chosen and titled "The Mind of the Church in the Formation of Sisters." Aware of opposition from within and without concerning this new thing called sister formation, the SFC leadership sought to position the work of the conference precisely on the directives of the Church. This move allayed the fears of many major superiors who thought that the new movement was against a tradition that had served religious communities well.

While the Church had long made recommendations for integrated pre-service education of sisters, nothing had specifically been legislated for sisters. Only by the "analogy of law" could sisters determine what directives were for them. "Canon 490, which states that the provisions of the law in which religious are named in the masculine gender apply equally to women religious, unless the contrary is obvious from the context or from the nature of the matter involved, also justifies our use of the analogy of law in the matter of Sister Formation."[6]

On the first day of the conference, bishops, priests, brothers, and sisters were to be invited to speak on various topics applying to the American scene: recent pronouncements of the Pope and the Congregation for Religious, ecclesiastical directives for seminaries and the education of religious men, sister education from the viewpoint of superintendents of schools, sister formation from the viewpoint of college and university administrators, and the formation program of religious communities of men. It was suggested that the keynote speaker for each of the six regions be the local bishop or his representative, again to bring validity to the meetings.

The second day of closed workshop sessions for the sisters was to be devoted to discussions on the talks given the day before, presentations of training programs already working in some women's communities, and a consideration of the proposed bylaws for a permanent Sister Formation Conference. Communities that included the baccalaureate degree for their beginning teachers were invited to share their formation programs.

Each regional chairperson was asked to schedule a regional committee meeting during July or August for the purpose of planning the region's own two-day conference. Sister Mary Emil, with Sister Ritamary attended each of these planning meetings to insure a unified approach to the conference days and a common understanding of the SFC and its purposes. In speaking of these meetings, Sister Ritamary said:

> We [Sister Mary Emil & Sister Ritamary] had borrowed a little bit of money from Msgr. Hochwalt to start the trip and we followed the regional setup of the NCEA, so that we contacted a superior in each place, who had tried to get a bishop or a superintendent of schools or someone who would be a diocesan authority, to come to these meetings and usually there would be something like 15 or 20 people and we just sat around a table and discussed what the movement was about, what its objectives were and that the research had shown that the superiors wanted to have their Sisters educated, but they were running into these obstacles; lack of personnel and lack of facilities . . . we would read and discuss some of the key passages from the Papal Directives. . . .It was all just a little tense because up to this time communities didn't meet together.[7]

The history of the SFC was given at these gatherings along with an explanation of the purpose of the Conference. It is quite correct to surmise that much evolutionary thinking was going on at this time. Every new question, suggestion, or meeting made the purpose of the SFC clearer to those who were leading and those who participated.

The first regional conferences more than met the expectations of the sisters. To the delight of all involved in the planning, a bishop in every geographical region sponsored the first set of conferences. Every response from a bishop was seen as an affirmation of the work being done and often bishops' letters were circulated among the national and regional chairpersons as a means of encouragement. Backing of the bishops was needed by the sisters and, though sometimes slow in coming, it was to guarantee the life of the conferences. Two hundred forty-six religious communities and 170 general or provincial superiors participated in the meetings. Reports came in from each region and showed the mix and variety of each region. One bishop in attendance claimed that he learned more about his sisters in one day than ever before. During one session, another bishop offered to defer the building of all new schools for a year so that adequate formation of the sisters could take place.

It should be noted that each conference was held at a college, again evidencing the continued support of higher education. One comment told of the impact of the regional conferences to set a direction for women religious:

In general it is safe to summarize those conferences by saying that speakers and Sister participants were pretty much of a mind that loyalty to the Holy Father and response to the needs of our times required that every community, in its own way and at the best rate consistent with its own situation and problems, should strive for the Bachelor's degree as a minimum educational training for a Sister, and for a juniorate to provide for spiritual formation continued after the novitiate.[8]

A reflection on the regional meetings was offered by Sister Mary Emil and revealed some of the internal tensions that had to be recognized and addressed in order to promote the idea of an integrated sister formation process.

In the first set of Sister Formation Conferences (1954-55) strong emphasis was put upon the education of Sisters--usually the college education of Sisters. . . . It is quite true that more was said about the importance of the B.A. than about the importance of mental prayer. This was not because planners or speakers thought the B.A. more important than mental prayer, but because they felt that there was a special urgency about remedying the low state of Sisters' studies and because some of them at least thought that if the Sister formation personnel of all kinds could be kept thinking and talking together long enough it might emerge that the B.A.and mental prayer were not totally unrelated.[9]

With the results of the regional conferences in hand, there was serious planning before the NCEA convention where planning on the national level took place. These meetings of the National Sister Formation Conference were open only to sisters and the 1955 NCEA Convention was the first gathering of major superiors, college personnel, and formation directresses. The topic discussed was graduate study for sisters. Aspects of the topic included the selection process used to determine which sisters should go on for graduate study, necessary arrangements for their studies, and how to use them once they returned to their communities. At this same convention the by-laws were approved and came to be known as the SFC regulations. Over 350 sisters attended this convention.

Along with discussing the bylaws and passing them to the executive committee of the department for approval, the official statement of the purpose of the Sister Formation Conference was also approved. All official publications of the movement would henceforth state: "The Sister Formation Conferences seek the advancement of the religious, cultural and professional formation of sisters, on preservice and inservice levels."[10] Because the work of the chairperson was increasing, Sister Mary Emmanuel Collins, OSF, was nominated for and elected to the office of vice-chairperson of the Sister Formation Conference.

Publications

In order to preserve and disseminate the ideas of the regional conferences, it was determined that the main ideas of the talks would be printed and circulated among religious communities, bishops, and others interested in a yearly volume. Though each year's title indicated the conference theme, the volumes received the generic title of "proceedings."[11] The addresses given on the first day of each of the Conferences were included and, due to the great similarity in all the regional programs, only excerpts of the other talks were reported. A $4000 grant from the Michael Grace II Trust in cooperation with Fordham University Press made the publication possible. The following is an evaluation of the first volume:

> The technical and educational discussions which were carried on during the first year of the group's history have been gathered together in a recently published book, *The Mind of the Church in the Formation of Sisters*. . . .It may well be one of the most significant books about Catholic Education in general and teacher training in particular that have been published in the United States. Opening with a letter from Valerio Cardinal Valeri, prefect of the Sacred Congregation for Religious, and a foreword by the Apostolic Delegate to the United States, the book in eight chapters lays the groundwork for a long-range program to improve the training and formation for the members of the various communities that have undertaken to cooperate in the study.[12]

Sister Mary Emil and her committee were concerned about keeping Rome as informed as possible since the approbation of Vatican agencies would give the Sister Formation Conference the seal of approval needed to sway some American bishops and religious superiors. Thus Sister Mary Emil queried:

> . . . let me say simply that I am wondering if anything at all could be achieved by a courtesy call on His Excellency, the Papal Delegate. I am thinking of a very brief visit, <u>with you</u>, to present him perhaps with a copy of our *Bulletin* and such programs as are printed by then, and to leave with him the impression that this movement, within the N.C.E.A., is a kind of mild American

counterpart of the professional federations of nuns which have been formed abroad, and wishes [sic] to indicate by this call that it is still very much within the Catholic Church.[13]

Copies of all published materials including the *Proceedings* were sent to the Congregation for Religious. Any letters of response were promptly printed in the *Bulletin* for all to see.

The *Sister-Formation Bulletin* served as an organ of communication for the Sister-Formation Conference. The first issue came out in October, 1954. The *Bulletin* was published four times a year by the Conference at a subscription price of 50 cents an issue. Its purpose was to "serve as publicity medium on new things in Sister-formation, wherever they may be taking place. Its scope extends to Sister formation in all its aspects--spiritual, intellectual, and professional training and their fitting integration in pre-service and in-service programs."[14] The organizational plan of each issue was the same. There was to be at least one article by an authority who addressed an area of sister formation, news sections on the regional and national sister formation conferences, reviews of articles and books that touched any aspect of formation, and news about sisters doing anything experimental.

Sensing the importance and impact of this publication, Sister Mary Emil and Sister Ritamary did everything possible from the very beginning to guide its purpose and content. Though Brother Bonaventure was the first major contributor, Msgr. Hochwalt's contribution was sought due to his position as general secretary of the NCEA. "For the first article in the first issue of the first volume we obviously need a contributor of first rank, and are therefore attempting to draft you."[15] The two topics suggested to Msgr. Hochwalt indicate the thinking of the early planners of the SFC:

A statement in which you set forth what you conceive to be the significance of this cooperation among the Sisterhoods in the field of Sister-Formation would be appropriate and effective. Or, you might develop the topic which we discussed in Washington and in which you expressed your interest--namely Sister-education as a specific type of education.[16]

The *Sister Formation Bulletin* was soon going into hundreds of convents and was being read communally and individually. ". . . 85 per cent indicated that they [general and provincial superiors] had recommended or prescribed the use of the *SF Bulletin* in all houses under their jurisdiction. From local superiors it was learned that 99.2 per cent are making the *Bulletin* available to all Sisters on the mission. Use of the *Bulletin* for public or general reading is a practice on 75 per cent of the missions."[17]   At first seen as an organ of limited circulation, the *Bulletin* soon changed its purpose from internal communication for superiors, novice directresses, and college personnel in charge of the education of sisters, to a vehicle for informing individual sisters, priests, and anyone interested in the formation of sisters.   There was concern over the financial losses incurred by a subscription rate of 50 cents.   It was determined, however, that the *Bulletin* must be continued and every effort would be made to increase necessary subscriptions. An interesting offer from Father Gerald Kelley of the *Review for Religious* to permit the *Bulletin* to become a department in the *Review* was declined. The sisters felt that since the *Bulletin* was the only publication of its kind and the official organ of the movement, everything should be done to keep it autonomous. At the time of the meeting with the National Consultative Committee of Sister Formation, the subscription price was raised to $1.00 and it was agreed that complimentary copies of the latest issue be sent to all vicars of religious with an accompanying note from the national committee urging them to subscribe.

According to Sister Mary Emil, the publication of the *Sister Formation Bulletin* was primarily the work of Sister Ritamary Bradley:

> At the time when I first interested her [Sister Ritamary] in this work I think it could safely be said that she was the most promising young scholar in any of our women's colleges . . . this sister has made the most noteworthy contribution to the <u>theory</u> of the movement.   There is an emerging philosophy of Sister Formation--and it owes more to Sister Ritamary than to anyone else.   Furthermore--she has made this theory understandable to and actually understood by the leaders in our communities of women.[18]

Sister Ritamary as the original editor and as the editor until 1964, established a high standard for acceptable articles.   She herself wrote for the *Bulletin* and was also able to do much of the translating required by articles from foreign countries. International exchange was begun with articles coming from France, Italy, and Canada.   Concurrently, Sister Ritamary continued a full-time teaching schedule along with other campus duties.   A fire in 1957 destroyed the motherhouse of the Sisters of Humility, in Ottumwa, Iowa, and with it all the early papers of the Sister Formation Conference, the manuscript for *Proceedings III* and the complete manuscript of community history that Sister Ritamary was writing.   Only in 1958 did another sister, Sister Gladys Marie, FCSP, begin to help her and this in the area of circulation.

In less than six months from the first publication in 1954, circulation of the *Bulletin* was up to 565 copies.   After the first mimeographed issue, it was necessary to have the following issues printed. The color blue was selected for the paper and it acquired the nickname "blue sheets." Communities were encouraged to subscribe for each of their houses and send complimentary copies to members of the clergy. It was understood and planned that members of the hierarchy would receive the *Bulletin*. This dissemination of information both internally to sisters and externally to publics interested in sisters became a most important tool of education. Sisters for the first time received first hand information on documents of the Church, talks directed to the topic of formation, research done by and for sisters, and the latest books for their enrichment. A high quality of spiritual and intellectual reading was being given to sisters. No longer were priest-authors directing what sisters would be reading, but sisters were determining what up-to-date material would be given to their fellow sisters. Soon, even the format of such periodicals for religious men and women as *Sponsa Regis* and *Review for Religious* took on different looks to meet the demand for intellectual reading. The *Bulletin* provided other services for sisters: reprints of talks given, tape recordings for contemplative communities, and a center for idea exchange.

A letter from Valerio Cardinal Valeri, Prefect of the Sacred Congregation for Religious, announced the special approval of the Sacred Congregation of Religious on the *Sister Formation Bulletin* and on the efforts of the Sister Formation Conference. Looked upon as a milestone, this letter was quoted in full in the June 1955 *Bulletin* and read to all at the 1955 NCEA convention.

Funding for Further Study

The Sister Formation Conference knew the importance of research in substantiating experienced reality, and a study of the practices of sister education in the United States and in Europe was deemed important to all future work. In order to do this, the National Sister Formation Committee sought corporate funding to help finance the research project. Sister Mary Emil pursued the possibility of getting a grant from the Ford Foundation to explore the relationship between liberal arts and professional studies in the training of sisters. The interest of the Ford Foundation was early evidenced.

Working directly with Dr. Alvin Eurich, who represented the Ford Foundation Fund for the Advancement of Education, Sister Mary Emil was early on encouraged to submit a proposal. Action, however, was delayed until after the 1955 NCEA convention as some National Consultants felt the SFC needed a better corporate status, and bylaws would be drawn up in the six regions by that time. There was also a concern that the proposed study might bring out publicly the weaknesses surrounding sister education in America.

Not until May 1955 did Sister Mary Emil and Sister Ritamary visit Dr. Eurich seeking funding for a three-stage study: 1) September 1955 through May 1956, several sisters would investigate current viable practices in sister education and needs for curriculum planning by means of personal interviews with communities. 2) June through August 1956, a committee of outstanding sister educators would live together and, with the help of special consultants, work at creating an ideal curriculum for the undergraduate studies. 3) October through February 1956-57, the dissemination of this information through the regional SFC Conferences would take place. Dr. Eurich supported the plan particularly because it sought to blend general and liberal arts training for future teachers, nurses and social workers. Fifty thousand dollars was sought for the project. In order to make the project totally acceptable, it was determined that the three-part study would have to be tied to a demonstration center. This stipulation posed no problem as such a center was the reason for even seeking to create a curriculum for sisters. Later was it announced that Sister Emmanuel Collins, OSF, vice-chairperson of the Sister Formation Conference and dean of the College of Saint Teresa, Winona, Minnesota, would participate in a fourth part of the project. Her community would allow her to spend the next year in Europe making a study of sister formation there.

Once the grant was given, Sister Mary Emil and Sister Xaveria began a journey of nine months of hard work. They were later joined by Sister Judith FCSP. Their tentative plan was to visit and consult at various universities during September and to use the remaining months for planning regional conferences and visiting of motherhouses and colleges. Time was also taken to gather a committee of outstanding sister educators. In September 1955, Sister Emmanuel began to study sister education in Europe. At this same time, an office had been made available in New York City for the use of the Sister Formation Conference through the courtesy of Francis Cardinal Spellman, archbishop of New York, Msgr. John J. Voight, and Father John P. Haverty, superintendent of New York Catholic schools.

1955-56 SFC Regional Conferences & NCEA Convention

The second series of the regional conferences, 1955-1956, sought to build on the work of the first. The theme selected was integration between the spiritual and intellectual formation of the sister. Though all the NCEA conference delegates approved of the idea, there was not yet much written about this theme and not everyone was convinced that integration of the spiritual and the intellectual was necessary or possible.

It was decided that an opinionnaire sent to a small number of priests in each region would help to gather 25 or 30 pages of information on different aspects of the theme. Hopefully, the theological and philosophical principles underlying each aspect could then be brought to light and the theme's credibility would be better established. The questions asked ranged from topics of intellectual and spiritual integration to spiritual formation. They gave an insight into the thinking of the SFC planners and reflected a certain stereotypical attitude about the place of women in the Church. Asking priests to comment on statements such as "many Sisters have a natural preference for domestic work and the interior decoration of schools and convents" and "women are more inclined to emotional piety--have less taste for solid doctrine"[19] found in the opinionnaire demonstrated that the sisters were aware of and perhaps even caught up in this attitude. Nevertheless, they wanted to develop the individual gifts of each sister with the new educational form they were recommending. This integrative formation would weaken the existing stereotype of the sister. Each region recorded its responses and circulated them among the sisters of the area. The sisters were encouraged to reflect on the responses and to share this thinking. Consciously or unconsciously, new ideas were spread.

It was decided that for the regional conferences, priest speakers would be featured during the morning of the opening day and sister speakers during the afternoon. Once again the second day would be closed to all but the official delegates. Workshop sessions were to be arranged in two ways: one in which administrators, formation personnel, and higher superiors were mixed together and the other in which each group met separately. One sister expert or consultant conversant in the topic would facilitate in each discussion group. The result was "substantial agreement at each of the six conferences that 'integration,' in the sense just described, was possible and desirable."[20] This integration was described as a harmony between the sister's personal religious life and her active apostolate. It was noted in the *Bulletin* that:

> The group discussions were much more effective this year, partly because the groups were smaller, and partly because of the splendid discussion guides given out in advance, giving participants an opportunity to prepare for participation in the discussions. A much better understanding of the Sister Formation movement, as well as a deeper appreciation of the work being done, and a seriousness of purpose seemed evident everywhere.[21]

The major talks of the regional conferences of 1955-56 were gathered together, edited by Sister Ritamary and printed in the second volume of the Proceedings, *Spiritual and Intellectual Elements in the Formation of Sisters*. This volume, with a foreword by Francis Cardinal Spellman and 38 papers on the conference theme, represented more fully the direct thinking of sisters as two-thirds of it was devoted to papers given by sisters. This pattern of sisters speaking to sisters about sister problems would become more pronounced. Also included were answers to the opinionnaire which had been sent to members of the clergy and the discussion guide used in the regional conferences. This volume, too, according to one observer, raised sister formation consciousness to a new level: "The discussion topics chosen are of the utmost importance and observations and reflections reproduced in this volume cannot but be of valuable assistance to Major Superiors in the weighty responsibility that is theirs to form their young religious according to the highest spiritual and intellectual standards."[22]

The 1956 NCEA meeting of the Sister Formation Conference centered on the general theme of "The Apostolate of the Teaching Sisters and the Problem of Time." Discussions on this topic were led by Sister Judith, FCSP, and Sister Elizabeth Ann, IHM, and centered around their studies on vocations and the in-service sister. Sister Mary Emil shared the progress of the first phase of the Ford Foundation study. Having traveled 28,000 miles to 83 different communities and 104 different places, she reported that 33 percent of the communities visited had lengthened their educational programs; 18 percent had plans to do so, and 36 percent favored a lengthened plan, leaving 13 percent with no definite plan. Over-all, superiors had expressed a sense of frustration heightened by the pressure of the state and its increased demands for certification, by varying interpretations of canon-law restrictions on studies for the young sister which seemed to be resolvable only by lengthening the whole training period, and finally by the pressure to send sisters out to serve in the schools. "It is a fact that children in our schools are increasing at the rate of 6.6 percent a year, and the Sisters in the active communities are increasing at the rate of 1.8 percent a year. It is conservative to say therefore that the elementary school population is increasing at least four times as fast as new recruits to the Sisterhoods can meet the demands for teachers."[23]

With much work to be done, the SFC looked hopefully to the activities of the next year. Preparations for the Everett Workshop were seen as a concrete step toward a practical and organized plan for an integrated educational experience for sisters.

1956-57 Everett Workshop, Regional Conferences, & NCEA Convention

During the summer of 1956, a special activity took the place within the Sister Formation Conference. With funding from the Ford Foundation, the SFC was able to sponsor a curriculum-planning workshop--the Everett Workshop (discussed in detail in Chapter III). This was the next logical step as superiors and directresses were looking for curricular patterns that would flesh out the ideals of sister formation. The Everett Workshop produced a liberal-arts-based undergraduate plan of studies for sisters. Before the 1956 NCEA convention, 3,000 copies of the report had been circulated to bishops, superiors of religious communities, college and university educators, and school superintendents.

It was decided that the regional conferences would use the results of the Everett Workshop as a starting point for discussion. Copies of the report of the Everett Curriculum were mailed in October to higher superiors taking part in the regional conferences. Priest speakers were asked to direct their comments to the topic, "New Horizons in Sister Formation," with the idea that all forms of the apostolate, not just teaching, would be addressed. One complication affected this year's meetings. A new decree now required the approval of the Congregation for Religious on programs and speakers for all meetings, conventions, or courses having to do with religious life. Some of the regional conferences were postponed until necessary permissions were received. The inconvenience the decree caused was probably not as great as the fear it appeared to spread among the members of the Sister Formation Conference. ". . . we shall all have to work together to correct any false impressions that may get about because of the postponement of the Conferences. . . .we cannot be too careful--as far as in us lies--to be sure that the postponement is understood for what it is."[24] When the SFC was advised that one person would have to act as a representative with Rome to arrange for the necessary permissions, the head of the college and university department was designated as a go-between. Despite a feeling of uncertainty caused by this new regulation, the *Bulletin* gave a public statement of Sister Formation Conference's allegiance to Rome:

> The decree itself is indeed ample evidence that the Holy See wishes the movement of renovation and adaptation of the States of Perfection to grow and to bear more abundant apostolic fruit. Sister Formation is proud to have been part of this world-wide movement and is eager to work in the closest and most faithful unity with it. The Sisters of the United States owe an incalculable debt of gratitude to Our Holy Father and the Sacred Congregation of Religious for calling attention to the need for better Sister formation and for encouraging initiatives such as those which have brought our conferences and *Bulletin* into being.[25]

The issue of authority was now in a bigger arena than when the Sister Formation Conference was first approved as a committee of the college and university department of the NCEA. In those early years, it was sufficient for the SFC to have its plans approved within the department. Now, deeper waters were being stirred, and it was being recognized that the SFC was moving in more than an educational circle. The 1956-57 Proceedings, *Planning for the Formation of Sisters*, centered on the work of the Everett Workshop. Along with a re-issued version of the results of the workshop, the volume contained the keynote talks of bishops in each region on the topic of the "Impact of a Changing Future on Sister Formation," and the thoughts of sisters speaking on the topics of expanded roles of sisters in the apostolate, conditions for intensifying the apostolate, and the spiritual formation needed for future apostolates.

SFC Receives Section Status

On 14 February 1957, the executive committee of the college and university department with the confirmation of the general executive board of the NCEA, granted the Sister Formation Conference the status of a section of the college and university department. The advance from a temporary committee to a permanent section gave the SFC the right to elect its own officers.

At the 1957 NCEA convention, the SFC delegates decided on the election procedures to be used. According to the revised regulations, all official delegates received nomination and election ballots by mail. The regional chairpersons would conduct the voting, with Mother M. Philothea, FCSP, at the head of the committee. The nine members of the Sister Formation National Committee were elected by the entire conference.

The SFC also asked at this time for a permanent secretariat; a sister formation office from where continuing study, research, and help could be coordinated. This secretariat was approved and the new headquarters were located in Washington, DC. The biggest problem recognized and addressed at this time aside from the need for expanded services to all communities was the need of the smaller community that did not have a college, the finances needed to provide for one, or the means to provide an adequate education for their sisters.

The 1957 NCEA Sister Formation program centered on the theme, "The Sister's Role in Preparing Youth for the Lay Apostolate." Sisters were not only encouraged to work with youth in order to prepare them for lay leadership in the Church, but also to acquire skills needed to do this kind of training. It was at this meeting that another landmark for the Sister Formation Conference was celebrated. In a letter addressed to Father Paul C. Reinert, SJ, president of the college and university department of the NCEA, and member of the National Sister Formation Consultative Committee, Cardinal Arcadio Larraona, CMF, secretary of the Congregation for Religious, publicly praised the work of the SFC and challenged it to both work with the Conference of Major Superiors of Women, CMSW, and to function within the NCEA. The letter was read at the opening session and the response to it was a motion that the SF Conferences send a cablegram to Cardinal Larraona thanking him for the recognition given to the

SF movement and the work of Sister Mary Emil. The SFC pledged to work with the CMSW and to remain loyal to the wishes of the Church.

Conference of Major Superiors of Women

Important in the history of the Sister Formation Conference was the formation in America of the Conference of Major Superiors of Women, CMSW, and its relationship to the SFC. As early as 1950 the Sacred Congregation had encouraged women religious throughout the world to organize into conferences of major superiors.

Already in 1952 Mother Gerald Barry, OP, was the chairperson of a committee established to investigate the possibility of such a conference for women religious in the United States and as such had headed the steering committee for the First National Congress of Religious in the United States, which was held at Notre Dame, 13 August 1952. During September of this same year the first congress of major superiors was held in Rome. Though it appeared that the work of the steering committee was over, it was the request of Father Arcadio Larraona, Secretary of the Congregation for Religious, that the committee remain intact. In December of 1955, Valerio Cardinal Valeri, Prefect of the Congregation for Religious, informed Mother Gerald that Father Bernard Ransing, CSC, representative of the Congregation for Religious, would be in the United States and wanted to meet with the committee" . . . to carry out the wishes of the Sacred Congregation for Religious to the extent at least, that you prepare the way for discussion of the formation of a conference of major religious superiors."[26]

The steering committee responded to Father Ransing by stating that they saw no necessity for such a conference of major superiors since they felt that other organizations in America such as the National Catholic Welfare Conference (NCWC) were adequately representing them.

> It was the consensus of the group that the services of NCWC should not be duplicated and negated the necessity of a conference of major superiors. The committee felt that the only organization that could be under the conference of major superiors would be the Sister Formation Conference, which was then a part of the National Catholic Association (NCEA) and, at the same time, under the education department of NCWC.[27]

It was in a talk given later in the year by Father Elio Gambari, SMM, of the Congregation for Religious that he explained how similar organizations existed in other parts of the world and once again how the Congregation for Religious

wanted such an organization that finally convinced the committee to go ahead
with plans. On 24 November 1956, a group of 235 major superiors approved the
formation of the Congregation of Major Superiors.

What to do with the SFC was a matter of discussion even while the
Conference of Major Superiors was still in the planning stages. There were
mixed feelings:

> Some committee members indicated that good work was being
> done by the formation group particularly in the area of curricula
> but others felt the group was infringing on the "jurisdiction" of
> major superiors by sending out questionnaires on religious life.
> They felt the group could assist major superiors but caution should
> be observed not to usurp their "jurisdiction."[28]

In December 1956, one month after the founding of the CMSW, Sister Mary
Emil wrote to the Sister Formation Committee explaining why it was so necessary
that the SFC become a section of the NCEA: "It seems to me that this is
absolutely necessary that something like this be done now to ensure that we will
go on, and to ensure that we can enter into some working relationship with the
Higher Superiors' Conference."[29] The thought and planning that went behind
this statement evidenced how badly Sister Mary Emil and the first leaders of the
SFC did not want the organization directly in the hands of the major superiors.
Now that the major superiors had their own organization, the SFC felt it was
imperative that they be protected further by sectional status in the NCEA and with
approval for independence from the Congregation for Religious.

> Sister Emil from the very beginning of SFC wanted the conference
> to be independent of the Major Superiors. She did not want it to
> be under the control of the superiors. In Canon Law, the superior
> always had the "last word" in any decision. The years 1956, 1957
> and 1958 were difficult ones. The Sister Formation Conference
> had already received approbation from the Sacred Congregation of
> Religious. In 1956, Rome had begun to establish throughout the
> world, Conferences for Major Superiors of Women and
> Conferences for Major Superiors of Men. Father Ransing was
> appointed by Cardinal Antoniutti as the liaison between the Sacred
> Congregation and the Conference for Major Superiors of Women
> in the United States. Both of them explicitly stated that the SFC
> was to be placed under the CMSW. Sister Emil disagreed with
> this arrangement and argued that the SFC had already been
> approved by Rome and therefore had priority to exist

independently.   Father Reinert, then President of St. Louis
University and a mentor of Sr. Emil, was involved in some of
these discussions.   Later in 1963 at the national meeting of the
CMSW, Archbishop Philippi, O.P., in a meeting with the ex-
officers of the CMSW and SFC told us that the problem really lay
in the fact that the "daughter (SFC) was born before the mother
(CMSW)."[30]

The recommendation of the Congregation for Religious as gleaned from
correspondence was that the SFC remain within the NCEA but under the
authority of the CMSW, and from the very beginning there was a tension between
the two groups. How to share responsibility in the strategic and sensitive area of
the formation of sisters was to be the critical issue.

Other Studies

In order to facilitate solid study and research in sister-education, the SFC
encouraged several sisters to examine the specific topics of vocations, juniorate,
in-service and Catholic women's colleges, and make their findings available to
sisters in America.

Sister Judith, FCSP, planned and directed a study that grew out of the work
of the 1954 Northwest regional SF Conference and became known as the
Vocation Survey. Fourteen thousand students in high school, college, and schools
of nursing, were asked to indicate their attitudes toward sisters. The results were
to help in understanding more about recruitment to religious life and provided
empirical evidence for the need for improved sister formation.

A project begun in 1955 by Mother Mary Florence, SL, concerned the study
of juniorates. Especially important to communities who were then contemplating
the opening of a juniorate, the data collected offered many suggestions.
Questionnaires were sent to all women's communities in May 1955 with
responses expected by June. Names of communities were not to be included. It
was promised that the complete report would be sent to all and the results were
published in the December 1955 issue of the *Bulletin*.

Yet another important work was begun by Sister Elizabeth Ann, IHM, when
she helped to organize "in-service committees" in each of the regions in 1955 so
that study and planning could begin for those sisters already working full-time.
This study foreshadowed the 1956 NCEA conference work on the in-service
needs of sisters. The Sister Formation Conference did not wish to ignore the
needs of these sisters yet recognized that they could at present handle only the
work of pre-service for sisters.

A second edition of the *Directory of Catholic Women's Colleges* was edited by Sister Gerard, OSF, and Sister Mary Basil, SSND, and published by the Bruce Company. At this time, there were still 118 communities with no educational facilities. This directory provided needed information for these communities and for those with special needs. Eighty-six women's colleges were listed as being willing to take sisters as students for greatly reduced rates and 30 full scholarships were offered. Copies were sent to 193 members of the hierarchy, 123 to diocesan superintendents, 550 to religious communities, and 253 to Catholic universities and colleges.

National Commission on Teacher Education and Professional Standards

The fact that Sister Formation Conference members were active and encouraged to join the Teacher Education and Professional Standards (TEPS) movement across the United States was both encouraging and challenging to the sisters. The ideas raised at these TEPS conferences had an influence on the sisters in their own efforts to create a sister-formation curriculum. As national chairperson, Sister Mary Emil represented the SFC at many TEPS meetings. "We are greatly pleased that you are going to be with us, and I hope that you will be prepared to give the Commission an overview of the developments in this field with your group; and that you not hesitate to point out, at appropriate times and places, just where the Commission can be helpful to your group."[31] wrote Dr. Stinnett to her.

As executive secretary of the National Commission on Teacher Education and Professional Standards, he contacted Sister Mary Emil 27 April, 1955, informing her that sisters representing the SFC would be welcome at the TEPS conferences along with representation from the NCEA. Sister Mary Emil had already attended the conference the year before and encouraged the sisters, if invited, to attend. The theme for 1955 was "Teacher Education: The Decade Ahead." The topics to be covered--curriculum, student personnel, post-graduate in-service--could have constituted the agenda for a SFC meeting. Ten members of the Sister Formation Conference received an invitation for the 1955 conference.

Various sisters were asked to give papers at TEPS conferences. The sisters were assured that their representation would be sought for all TEPS meetings. Such an open invitation was encouraging to this group of women seeking to upgrade the professional standing of their own group. The influence of TEPS on producing a curriculum for sisters was great and will be evident later in a more detailed account of the Everett Workshop.

Conclusion

As the Sister Formation Conference completed its first three years of existence, it had moved from a temporary committee to the status of a section of the NCEA. This move gave sisters in the conference independence in electing their own officers. Sister Mary Emil, this time by election, remained in command with the new title of executive secretary. The SFC leadership had decided during this time that priority would be given to six activities: travel for evaluating the Everett Report, attendance at the regional conferences; study of available help from Catholic and other agencies; looking into available scholarships and fellowships; keeping higher superiors informed about SFC; and seeking necessary Foundation funds to further the training of sisters. Each of these activities was promoting sister education in its own way. Religious across the United States and even Canada were coming to a better understanding and appreciation of their role in the work of the Church. Pastors and bishops were becoming aware of the financial burden all this training was placing on religious communities and were attempting to help. Lay people were also involved in sponsoring various activities for the needs of the sisters and supporting them in many other ways.

The work of the SFC did not move along without misunderstandings and opposition. The battle of intellectualism vs. spirituality was to be brought out in the open and became the bottom line issue of the Everett Workshop. Clergy, sisters and laity had their questions about this new idea of sister formation. The next years would be plagued with the task of trying to adequately define what types of formation the SFC was attempting to promote, a combination of which would allow for every sister to have a degree before assuming a position in the Church's ministry. It was a plan that would take into consideration all areas of formation: the spiritual, intellectual, social, apostolic, and professional. No longer was it sufficient to believe that being a sister in and of itself was enough to accomplish any task. "Yet another class of 'diehards' holds to the conviction that a Sister poorly prepared for teaching or nursing is better than no Sister at all; that the religious vocation itself will serve to cover--or cover up--a multitude of professional deficiencies."[32]

Sister Mary Emil struggled further with the balancing of pastoral needs and the needs of the sister for integrative formation, a situation daily thrown up to the SFC. If there were already so few sisters and a greater need for sisters every day, how could the SFC justify asking communities to delay the entry of sisters into the apostolate for as long as five years in order to be better formed? Looking at the long and arduous formation program already set in place for religious communities of men, Sister Mary Emil challenged the opposition to consider why religious women had not received the same kind of training as religious men.   She determined that more research needed to be done to determine if better sister formation would provide for better service.

> The possible role of the Church, of Catholic education, of Catholic Action, and of the teaching Sister as a first line fighter in the troubled years ahead of us--all of these must be realized. . . .Can we expect all this from Sisters whose sketchy training has spread over most of a lifetime, who have trouble sometimes in manifesting competence in the narrow subject-matter areas to which they have been assigned, and who are usually so overburdened with an excess of duties and charges and a cluttered horarium that they have no time or hardly time to be civil to the students, to say nothing of "inspiring" them? . . . Now it is the opinion of the writer that we will solve the vocation problem when we turn into the classroom, the nurses' training school and the hospital, dynamic, challenging, inspired, highly competent, and obviously happy and holy Sisters.   It is the further conviction of the writer that the production of such Sisters is a matter of longer and better training--spiritual, cultural and professional.[33]

The relationship of the Sister Formation Conference with the Conference of Major Superiors of Women was yet to be determined.   The SFC had set up its membership as including the leadership, the formation directresses, and the education directress of each community.   Those communities with colleges of women were encouraged to have the college president attend.   The object of the meetings was to bring about an integrative approach to sister formation.   The pattern set by the SFC of having the leadership, formation, and education segment work together hinted early at the concept of shared responsibility and planning, with no one area of authority overpowering the other.   The Conference of Major Superiors of Women had membership limited to major superiors.   The voices among major superiors who felt that the SFC was overstepping its bounds by advocating new formation practices and thus taking authority away from the role of the major superior would now have a hearing within a group made up totally of sisters in leadership positions.   An out-and-out struggle was certain to result. The SFC had accomplished great strides as a grass roots movement and now had to learn how to deal with a new organization of religious superiors, the CMSW. The question was whether the two groups could live and work side by side for the benefit of sisters.   A delineation of tasks would be necessary.

From "Operation Bootstrap" to "Operation Airlift" a solid foundation had been laid.   Religious communities were on the way to becoming more self-directed and their sisters more professionally ready.   "Sister Lucy" was gradually being recognized, not only as a teacher to be trained but as a person to be formed. Comments in the *National Catholic Educational Bulletin* were almost prophetic:

> Operation Bootstrap, with the grace of God, will succeed. It may perhaps take ten or fifteen years--not a long time in Church history. But as one travels around the country to see the valiant women who make up the American Sisterhoods doing a great self-sacrificing, dedicated work, but with all of that struggling against huge and remediable obstacles of inadequate time inservice, and inadequate formation preservice, one is continually saddened by the spectacle of how their apostolic efficacy could be multiplied NOW. . . .In the matter of collegiate Sister education, we have no wish for uniformity or the interference with internal government to which formation is canonically assigned, but the superiors themselves feel an urgent need for help with their planning and for a general and sympathetic understanding of what they wish to give the Sisters. Such a climate of opinion is the second future one could foresee for Sister formation--one which would turn Operation Bootstrap into Operation Airlift, and which could change the face of the active works in which the Sisters engage, not in fifteen years, but in five or six.[34]

CHAPTER III   EVERETT WORKSHOP

The three-part study financed by the Ford Foundation which was mentioned earlier as the Everett Workshop, was done with the purpose of exploring the relationship between liberal arts and professional studies in the training of sisters. The importance of the liberal arts and the desirability of equipping sisters to handle the future needs of the Church undergirded the attention given to the content of a college program for sister education. This program came to be known as the Everett Curriculum, named after the geographic place where the formative workshop took place.

The time was ripe and the forces were ready to abandon the patterns of an outdated educational system and to study and implement an integrative form of learning for the education of sisters. It was with a directed forcefulness that the National Sister Formation Committee in consultation with and approval of the National Consultative Committee sought to create a curriculum model that would allow the old educational customs to be replaced by a curriculum plan that would consider the total needs of the sister based on the needs of the changing world.

Serious study and research made obvious to sisters in America and to those interested in their training that past patterns no longer met the demands of state certification. With the same energy that motivated the actions of the first years of the Sister Formation Conference, a way was sought to create a viable curriculum model for the modern sister. This sister would have to meet the challenge of integrating her spiritual life with her apostolic work and her intellectual pursuits. This policy was to be the key of the entire Sister Formation Conference. Seeking to concentrate on the goal of total education of the person--a true integration of the spiritual, intellectual, professional and apostolic aspects of religious life--the SFC sought to prepare an integrated minister for the Church. Those attending the 1955-1956 SFC regional conferences struggled with the kind of balance that was needed between intellectual acumen and humility as they discussed and studied the theme of spiritual and intellectual formation. The work of the Everett Workshop was based on the fundamental belief that a well-

55

developed intellectual life would be a source of strength for any type of apostolic activity. The product of this total education was to be a sister who was spiritually enriched, "psychologically mature, intellectually disciplined, broadly cultured and professionally competent."[1] With an eye to the needs of America and American Catholics, the leaders of the SFC envisioned sisters who as teachers, nurses, and social workers, would stimulate the faith of many. Sr. Mary Emil remarked:

> The Everett project began with some of us who were teachers, back in 1954. Very simply, we were dissatisfied with the quantity and quality of the education the teacher members of our religious orders were getting. We saw two villains in the piece. One was grossly insufficient curricular planning. The other was the multiplication of state certification requirements in professional education. So we applied to the Ford Foundation for a grant to visit teacher-preparing institutions to find out to what extent they did think [sic] the professional requirements excessive, and to gather background material for the construction of a model curriculum of our own.[2]

The Ford Foundation grant had made the preliminary work on this formation program possible. The amount requested and received from the Ford Foundation was $50,000. The grant covered four stages of research:

1. September 1955 through May 1956: an exploration of the current and most effective practices in sister education in the United States and Europe.
2. June through August 1956: drawing up an ideal curriculum on the B.A. level by a committee of selected sister educators.
3. October 1956 through February 1957: regional SFC conferences to discuss the summer's work.
4. Post August 1956: a cooperative project in which a religious community or two would try out the new curriculum to show the validity of the research.

The Sister Formation Conference in planning for this curriculum project did not envision one set norm for sister education to be followed by all but rather foresaw a model that could be helpful, adopted and adapted by each community according to need. The SFC sought to work with each religious congregation where it was and hoped that by providing a model and even demonstration centers, better formation and educational programs would be promoted. Aware that state certification boards often determined what a community's educational program contained, the hope now was that an ideal curriculum pattern that encompassed and recognized certification needs would be the norm. No longer eager to have outside forces determine the content and type of education, the conference leaders wanted to create a curriculum that was styled for the needs of sisters.

Exploration and Preparation

Stage one of the research began immediately in September 1955 with an advance of money from Cardinal Spellman, who also offered an office for the SFC in the New York Archdiocesan Educational Building. Nine months were to be spent consulting with various university people, attending the regional conferences, and visiting religious communities in America.

During the first months, the travelling team was made up of Sister Mary Emil, IHM, and Sister Xaveria, IHM. The sisters met with college and university educators to seek advice and direction. They kept the National Sister Formation Committee and the National Consultative Committee informed of their program through periodic general letters that stated their progress. In seeking advice from lay and religious educators on both public and private university campuses, the sisters (both having doctoral degrees and college experience) displayed genuine openness and a great desire to establish a norm based on consensus. The advice they sought concerned sister education and the make-up of the upcoming curriculum workshop. As they visited Saint Louis University, Catholic University of America, University of Minnesota, and Marquette University, the two sisters more clearly understood what academic fields needed to be represented in a well-rounded curriculum, which sisters should be asked to participate in the workshop, and in what areas outside consultants would be most helpful. Further advice was received concerning certification, the need to obtain more funding from foundations, and the raising of standards in Catholic schools. Many educators consulted at this time would subsequently be consultants to the summer workshop.

Travelling in a car named "Raphael," Sister Mary Emil and Sister Xaveria, later joined by Sister Judith, IHM, traversed 44,268 miles through forty-four states. The majority of the time was spent visiting religious communities. Having received invitations from over one hundred-twenty major superiors desiring more discussion and an opportunity to plan, these sisters visited as many as they could.

> What we found would make your hair stand on end. For example, down in Louisiana there is a Congregation. . . .Their salary was $45 a month and that was common. . . .we asked how they were

preparing their sisters to go into these classrooms: they were going out immediately, almost as novices, and the superior with a terrible pained look said, "The superintendent says if they have had a fourth grade education themselves, they can teach second grade." And that's what they were doing.[3]

Fifty-two percent of the communities visited were involved in various ministries, and it was soon realized that the curriculum to be created had to consider the needs of all sister professions. Already in 1955, the SFC National Committee had been expanded to include a sister representative from the field of nursing and social work. Early in the planning for the workshop, it was decided that the proposed Sister Formation curriculum would have to be broad enough to benefit a sister of any apostolic work. "It was generally agreed that the specific roles of the sister teacher, nurse, social worker need to be more clearly defined. Participants were asked to study these roles in an effort to better identify the knowledge, skills and abilities needed by the sister as a sister in her professional work."[4]   Since superiors visited felt a strong need for mutual understanding among sisters in various professions, it was recommended that a common education would help to make this possible. The three professions in which most sisters worked: education, nursing and social work were found to have great similarity.

As in the earlier survey research, the visitation pointed up great educational diversity. This situation often was complicated by the great variety in educational entrance requirements. In certain parts of the United States, postulants who had not completed high school were admitted and sent out to teach before they had completed high school. Yet other communities required that the postulant complete her second year in college before being admitted. Most required the completion of high school before entering.[5]

It was also evident from the visits that there was still a lack of coordination between religious communities and Catholic colleges. As the sisters visited areas, they were often able to facilitate some arrangements between a religious community and a neighboring college. Factors such as distance from a college and financing kept some communities from educating their sisters, so the SFC encouraged communities with colleges to give scholarships to these communities.

The thought of an exclusive curriculum to train this cadre of women appealed to eighty-eight percent of the communities seen during the previous months. Eight percent thought there was no need for a curriculum different from that offered their lay counterparts and four percent were undecided. Responses to the type of environment in which sisters would be educated indicated polarities. Seventy-seven percent were in favor of a totally or at least partially separated educational environment for sisters. This thinking rested on the hope that a controlled environment would allow for a special kind of integrated formation that would not be possible if lay students were present. Twenty-three percent opposed this stand: ". . .they wished the young Sisters to be in class with seculars, for the sake of challenge, or for convenience and economy of administration."[6] Never a settled topic, the education of sisters isolated from the laity would be a point of contention that would eventually be a reason for the closing of most "sister-only" institutions.

> It is my impression that more is gained than lost in having the students go to class with other students. There is a subtle intra-group competition which puts a different kind of social pressure on the students when in separate classes. . . .The shape of the Catholic school is going to change drastically in the near future. The plausibility of continuing a separate system is being discussed more and more by literate laymen.[7]

A formal report on these community visits with a sharing of facts and recommendations would be made at the Everett Workshop.

The European scene was being covered by Sister Emmanuel Collins, OSF, dean of the College of Saint Teresa, Winona, Minnesota. Sister Emmanuel joined the project when she offered to study sister formation programs in Europe during the 1955-56 school year while she was a companion to a fellow sister studying in Europe.[8] A personal blessing of the Holy Father was obtained on the SFC and its work when Sister Emmanuel was able to visit with him on her tour. Sister Emmanuel observed that American sisters enjoyed more respect and admiration from the people of the United States than European sisters did from their people. Poorer for the most part than their American counterparts, European sisters in trying to take care of their own basic needs did not have as much time to work for and reach out to people as American sisters did. European sisters had fewer positions of authority as most educational institutions were run by the clergy. Though some communities had juniorates, and federations of sisters in Europe were beginning, it was generally felt that the European sister was under more constraints. Though many religious communities serving in America had roots in Europe, the culture of America had definitely thrust the sister into a different mode of living. In America, sisters built and staffed most of the Catholic institutions for education, social work, and health care.

While the sisters were travelling in America and Europe, major decisions concerning participants, location, and demonstration centers had to be made in preparation for the Everett Workshop. The search for workshop participants took place during the fall and spring of 1955 and 1956. Two qualities were expected of each participant: a doctoral degree with some publications or outstanding work in one's field and a strong belief in sister education.[9]

> They must be creative and courageous. They must be determined to uphold academic standards, but they must also be in sympathy with our ideal of integrated formation. . . .As far as possible they should represent different communities, different geographic areas, and different kinds of undergraduate and graduate training.[10]

Working closely with the National Consultative Committee, Sister Mary Emil was authorized to begin contacting possible participants to fit broad academic areas:

> I reported that after assembling all the advice received at the universities and from the Sisters, I could propose the following list of academic areas to be represented by the sixteen national participants at the workshops: Education (2), Philosophy (2), mathematics, English (2), Psychology, Theology, History, Fine Arts, Languages, Economics, Sociology, Physical Sciences, Biology. . . .I then submitted a list of names with proposals which have come in from all sources. . . .They [national consultants] went over them field by field with much interest and authorized me to proceed on contacting Sisters or running down leads.[11]

Aside from determining who would be a part of the workshop, much energy was also used in deciding the right place to hold the meeting. The Providence School of Nursing, operated by the Sisters of Providence in Everett, Washington, was finally chosen because of Everett's closeness to important education meetings scheduled during the workshop session, (TEPS, NCATE, and state-certification officers would be in the area and therefore available to the sisters for consultation) and because of the state's climate and scenery. Disadvantages such as the lack of library facilities and the absence of an academic atmosphere were dismissed by the national consultors. That the libraries of Washington University, the University of Seattle and the University of Portland would be available would suffice. It was also seen as an advantage to be away from a campus atmosphere "to be absolutely free in our thought."[12]

The two communities chosen to implement the curriculum in demonstration centers were the Sisters of Saint Francis of Rochester, Minnesota (College of Saint Teresa) and the Sisters of Providence, Seattle, Washington (Providence Heights College). The campuses were chosen from a number of possible options by a vote of the National Sister Formation Consultative Committee. The process had not been open to many communities. "It was not judged wise to contact all the congregations in the country, in view of the need for haste and the difficulty in explaining the proposition by mail, but there seems to be no doubt that very many congregations would be intensely interested in a project of this sort."[13]

The College of Saint Teresa, operated by the Sisters of Saint Francis, had been a fully accredited liberal arts college since 1917. Though the main campus of the college is located in Winona, an extension exists at the motherhouse in Rochester. The fact that Sister Emmanuel, the dean of the college, was already engaged in research for this project, both with European travel and study and as a participant in the Everett Workshop, was obviously a key factor in the choice of the College of Saint Teresa. Sister Emmanuel was also the vice-chairperson of the Sister Formation Conference at this time.

The Sisters of Providence of Seattle, also vitally interested and active in the Sister Formation Conference were selected because of their plans to create something new in sister education. Sister Judith Lang, FCSP, who had already shown leadership in the SFC, was selected to direct the new curriculum project in her community. An entirely new college was to be built and its faculty was to be trained to the doctoral level at various universities in selected areas. The plans of the congregation were that all sisters were to receive a liberal arts background. After receiving a degree, a fifth year of study in a professional field at another university was to yield a master's degree. Cooperation with Seattle University would be sought while Providence College was being built. It was hoped from the start that the two demonstration centers would be show places for sister education. It was felt that progress could be monitored and that the concrete example of Saint Teresa and Providence Heights would provide an irresistible example.

Mind-Set, Methods, Considerations

Though the Everett Workshop was called "a curriculum construction project,"[14] the gathering had a greater impact than that title indicated. Here was an assembly of educated women meeting with the blessing of the Catholic Church and financed by American industry for the purpose of planning the educational future of the American woman religious. The goals of the Everett Workshop and objectives of the curriculum openly acknowledged that past training patterns could no longer meet today's certification demands.

That she [the sister] be psychologically mature, intellectually disciplined, broadly cultured, and professionally competent is mainly the objective of the academic programs. . . .Translated into areas of study these would include a strong background in theology and philosophy, a broad foundation in the humanities and the natural sciences, mastery of the arts of communication, and a planned sequence in psychology and the social sciences.[15]

It was believed that the sister and all of religious life would be transformed by this sister education and that there would be an increase of vocations because of the influence of sisters formed by such a program. Lastly, it was felt that there would be an extension of works of mercy because the sisters would be more skilled in their fields.

The sister participants, many of whom had participated in the major meetings of the Sister Formation Conference, came prepared to work and had shipped their reference materials ahead of them. The next logical step was preparing a curriculum guide. The assembly worked toward a curriculum that would gather and refine principles that could be used in constructing a pattern of sister education that would have a profound effect on American society. That this was to be an educational plan that would afford sisters a better education than the ordinary laywoman was stated early in the workshop.

The necessity of an education better than the ordinary was based on the belief that sisters were to be in the forefront of Church work and service and were to do it better than anyone else. It was believed that the sister of tomorrow would have to be educationally equal with the lay teacher; that she would have to grasp the importance of her leadership role in the Church and in Catholic education; and that she would be expected to direct all her talents toward these goals. Therefore, the sister of tomorrow needed a knowledge of the social principles of the encyclicals so that she could teach the young and work with adults in the reconstruction of the social order. It was predicted that the sister would be expected to lead and train leaders for Catholic action, adult education, community colleges, and CCD work. Sister Mary Emil would term it as "having a quasi-share in the magisterium"[16] of the Church and that a better education than the ordinary laywoman was the only way to be prepared to serve adequately. This view of the future works of the American woman religious cast her into new roles of active leadership, leadership she had consistently taken in the past and now would be prepared for. Reconstruction of the social order was seen as critical for America as it attempted to recover from a World War and a Cold War and to cope with the threat of communism and the national unrest of racial difficulties.

It was generally agreed that the sister had to be a competent professional as well as a holy religious. Therefore, the socially adjusted and competent teacher, social worker, or nurse was the joint goal of this spiritual and intellectual training. To synthesize the sister's education, formation and the apostolate was the goal of the workshop participants.

The established order of the day devoted the mornings to sharing sessions, set aside the afternoons for research, study, and writing and ended each day with a sharing meeting in the evening. In order to complete the work in three months, the sisters worked six days a week. A day was allotted to each academic field for presentation and discussion. As part of her preliminary homework, each sister was expected to consult authorities in her field in order to decide the best possible contributions to an undergraduate program. It was determined that the contributions from the various fields should be made with an emphasis on curricular patterns and that all recommendations be as practical and realistic as possible. The content, sequence of courses, and knowledge and competencies of each field were considered. Minutes of the daily meetings were duplicated for the workshop participants.

The first formal report concerned the gathered information of the travelling team. Over 53,000 sister contacts had been made during the United States trip, and the comments gathered concerned the length of time and kinds of study done in formation, educational practices and opportunities offered, future plans, and needs felt by each visited community.

Gleaned from the informal minutes of the Everett Workshop are these recommendations made to the workshop group after a study of the visitation report:

1. Provide a five year program of training for young sisters.

2. Recommend college work through the bachelor's degree before sending the sisters into professional work such as teaching, nursing, social work.

3. Place less emphasis on the purely professional and on more on the educational.

4. Emphasize joint planning of curriculum by personnel of the novitiate, college and those concerned with sister formation and education.

5. Advocate a study of the abilities and interests of the individual sister in order to determine the placement of the sister.

6. Affirm the release of sisters full time to develop their overwhelming abilities, e.g., writing, research.

7. Prepare elementary teachers to teach a foreign language in the grade school.

8. Structure campus elementary schools with a forward look and prepare to carry out experimental programs.
9. Promote community planning that includes plans for financing the programs.
10. Stress special educational practices that include plans for graduate work for sisters able to undertake this study, including a year's study abroad.
11. Explore cooperation in the education of sisters with other communities.
12. Organize real curriculum planning and research. Plan for philosophy, theology, and social science courses in the curriculum. Devise a number of special courses geared to sisters' needs. Use television, music, and dancing in novitiates. Specially train faculties for the education of young sisters.
13. Complete curriculum reevaluation and planning.
14. Start graduate study in juniorate.
15. Certify all teaching sisters whether certification is required or not.
16. When sisters are attending regular community colleges for women, establish special sections with well thought-out programs for them.[17]

The participants and consultants depended heavily on research to document the needs of the present day. No decisions would be made concerning the content of courses, placement in the curriculum or sequence until these studies were done. As trends were cited, pertinent applications were made toward an adequate curriculum. The sisters in the workshop studied the effects of industrialization, communication, and urbanization. Population increase in the Third World, computerized living and automation, changes in the labor picture, the impact of mass culture and mass media, a religious reawakening, and the needs of the Third World were also examined. Rather than being simply reactors to situations, these sisters hoped to be in a position to act and plan particularly for their future and the type of service they would be able to render to the Church. The interest of religious communities to study various educational patterns was growing. Not only were communities more ready to work together but they were also beginning to realize that outside forces were having an effect on curriculum patterns and that changes needed to be made. With an eye to the future, they wanted sisters to have the best preparation possible for various assignments to the works of the Church in the society of tomorrow. These sisters felt that the sister of tomorrow would be linked in a strong way to the American suburban life. It had been hoped that there would also be a revival of the American family and new opportunities for political and economic group action. The growth of the civil rights movement and the formation of the peace corps came during the 1960's. Signs of great unrest were appearing on college and university campuses. If nothing else, it was certain that the social structure of America was about to change.

The workshop group also recognized the changing form of teacher education. Already teacher education groups were stating that a five-year program was needed so that professional work could take place on the foundation of a four-year liberal arts education. There was a growing trend toward student teaching taking place over an extended period. Even the teaching of moral and spiritual values was observed as a new need on all levels of education.

Yet another concern for the workshop members was their relationship to state certification officers. Invited to explain the Everett project at the National Association of State Directors of Teacher Education and Certification (NASDTEC), a group of nine sisters led by Sister Mary Emil represented sister formation concerns to those officers meeting at Pacific Lutheran College, Parkland, Washington, 24-26 June 1956. The intent of the visit was to demonstrate the difficulty experienced by three-fourths of all sister teachers who taught in more than one state and had to meet the multiple and detailed certification requirements of each state.

The Everett Workshop was only in its third week when this meeting took place. This drafted message to the wider SFC demonstrated the direction these sister educators were advocating:

> We wish to speak as a group of college people working against a background of certain research and having the authority simply of such research and of our own academic competency. Our message to NASDTEC is double:

> We would like to corroborate, from our special point of view, the point already made by others, that the ideal arrangement in teacher certification is certification upon recommendation of an approved teacher-training college.

> In the interim we would ask consideration of the position of the colleges which might wish to recommend for

certification Sister students educated according to the experimental patterns proposed at the Everett workshop.[18]

The purpose of the meeting was to win early approval for the use of the Everett curriculum in colleges for sisters, approval that would satisfy certification requirements. The SFC group made it clear that the Everett participants had done very serious study on the matter of certification and that any professional consideration of the new sister curriculum would be appreciated. Along with working with this certification group, they wanted to support and cooperate with the National Commission on Teacher Education.

The sisters informed the certification officers of their research and the study that was resulting in a curriculum that would have fewer professional courses but a stronger liberal arts base. Though no decisions were made at this joint meeting, it was felt that the plight of the sister teacher working in various states was better understood. Also the certification officers requested that they receive a copy of the Everett Curriculum for their further discussion.

The Curriculum Report

The contents of the Everett Report began with an introduction by Sister Mary Emil. In it she explained that the proposed curriculum would improve the quality of instruction in the schools and, therefore, have a profound effect on American society. It was reiterated that the purpose of the workshop had not been to arrive at a single pattern of sister education but rather to assemble and refine principles which any solid pattern of sister education should take into account. "It is hard to say how many congregations will adopt the specific implementation of these objectives in our curriculum. That depends on the kind of job which is done, and on the success achieved by the demonstration centers."[19]

"The Situation in Sister Education," the topic of chapter one, considered the needs and practices in education; technological and social horizons; and new horizons in education. The goals of the Everett Workshop and objectives of the curriculum were covered in the second chapter. Here the challenge of meeting the needs of tomorrow was stressed and discussed.

The chapter on academic fields covered each discipline and presented the rationale for including it in the educational pattern of the curriculum. A more detailed explanation was given of those fields considered the foundation bed of the Everett Curriculum. Theology was viewed as a distinct discipline that provided a solid foundation for the spiritual life of the sister along with a particular preparation for her apostolic work. Philosophy was to give the sister a general framework for understanding all she was to learn. The sequence of theology and philosophy was the core of this curriculum. Among the other disciplines, sociology was to foster an understanding of the social forces that the sister would need to deal with and an understanding of the social doctrines of the Church. Economics was to help the sister be receptive to the needs of varying age and income groups. Political science was to help her assess political issues. Psychology was given a special place in this curriculum and was viewed as important for the assimilating of those facts, theories, and principles so important for the understanding of the person. It was held that if emotional maturity was to be the foundation for spiritual formation, psychology could give the sister an idea of the kind of balance needed for integrated development. Although the psychology of woman was never specifically mentioned at Everett, it was Sister Mary Emil who explained that there was a psychology of sisters as sisters. "We did feel that the Sisters are a special group and this had implications both for content and slant in the curriculum. . . .I don't think that women as women have ever been called upon to realize the distinctive contribution they could make to scholarship."[20]

The three main professions of teaching, nursing, and social work were covered in chapter four. With an emphasis on how preparation for these professions could be enhanced by following the Everett Curriculum, this chapter served as a guide to communities involved in various ministries.

Chapter five concentrated on how the two demonstration centers, Saint Teresa College and Providence Heights, were going to adapt the Everett Curriculum. The curriculum pattern for both colleges was basically the same yet shaped for the needs of the religious communities served. Since the College of Saint Teresa was an established college for lay women and had served sisters of various communities for many years, the Everett Curriculum served as a guide for a renewed model of education for sisters. The College of Sister Formation at Providence Heights was a new college for sisters only and an institutional branch of Seattle University.[21]

The concluding chapter addressed problems relating to the organization, instruction, and administration of sister education. The details enumerated became the basis of the work to be done by religious communities. The importance of the training of teachers for sister colleges was also set out in this chapter. No matter how wisely or carefully constructed the curriculum might be, it would be totally ineffective in the hands of a faculty that did not understand the implications of the curriculum. Several recommendations were made to communities eager to set up a system of excellent education:

1. Plan and implement a curriculum that is intellectually rich.

2. Arrange an exchange program by which faculty members may have an opportunity to teach in another college.
3. Encourage faculty members to join faculties of other colleges in cooperative studies, conferences, and to become members of learned societies.
4. Create a good library.[22]

The concerns were focused on by the SFC over the next years. As communities actively sought to establish a satisfactory form of sister education, the norms established by the work of the Everett Workshop set up a criteria or checklist to be followed. The regional conferences would be seen as the practical way to educate the religious communities to these new criteria and norms.

Regional Conferences

The purpose of the regional conferences for 1956-57 was the dissemination of the Everett Report with an "accurate assessment of the Sisters' present situation and status and of bold prophecy of their future place in the American church."[23] The SFC invited priests, bishops, college administrators, and superintendents of schools to share their insights concerning the social, cultural, technological, and religious changes that they foresaw would affect the apostolate of sisters. Participants in this set of regional conferences came away convinced that the Sister Formation Conference was not satisfied with saying the Everett Curriculum was the last word in sister formation but, that fitted to the needs of the Church, it could be effective. Major superiors were challenged to look beyond the present situation and status of sisters to an accurate and expanding picture of the future place of women religious in the American Catholic Church.

Practical input at the regional conference was information gathered from recent studies conducted by sisters concerning finance, the professional needs of in-service sisters, and the status of sister teachers.[24] With frightening accuracy the America of tomorrow was placed before the sisters in attendance. It was demonstrated that by 1971 there would be more lay teachers than sisters in the Catholic school system. The question posed to sisters was whether they would be ready to be a minority group of teachers in what were thought to be their own schools. The question posed to Catholic people was whether they would be able to adjust quickly enough to the new situation and new way of financing Catholic schools. Future planning was no longer a recommendation; it was a necessity for survival. Sisters were urged to investigate alternate apostolates beyond the work in a single parish school. It was noted that unless more sisters got into high school and undergraduate education, the education of women would be held down. Another apostolate seen as viable for the needs of tomorrow was that of early childhood education. The apostolate of the university professor in the capacity of scholar, writer, and researcher was also advocated. Interestingly, Sister Mary Emil noted that perhaps few sisters were in these positions due to a fear that the training required would "engender pride and be a divisive force in our congregations," and she went on to say that failure to allow qualified sisters to go on is a denial of the talents of the sisters and needs of the Church. Catholic action and CCD work were two other apostolates seen as places where the influence of sisters should be felt.

Certainly the sense of internal isolationism that had been a part of religious life for sisters was being challenged. "Surely in this age of the lay apostle, finding our proper role would mean that we would realize that it is our mission to train the lay apostles, and that this will require us to be super-apostles--women of great competence and greater spirituality."[25] Sisters were asking sisters and all in the Church to look ahead and plan. Responsibility for this type of foresightedness was placed squarely on the shoulders of the higher superiors, local superiors, and the sister herself. This challenge to the individual sister--unknown in these years of corporate thinking--was given when Sister Mary Emil insisted that every individual sister know what was going on in the apostolate, whether she was a novice or had been in the community for many years. The common life "of regulated behaviors and work that functioned to maintain the institution but not necessarily to bring each woman to fullness of human growth and potential"[26] was giving way to a new interpretation of personal responsibility.

Conclusion

The work of the summer was finished and after several revisions the Everett Curriculum was ready for publication. The students who would be following the curriculum were to be a hand-picked, highly motivated group. The curricular program had been refined to a system of integrative learning based on a solid core of philosophy and theology taught in a sequence that formed the foundation upon which a social science and psychology sequence could be placed. The liberal arts were represented by courses in the humanities, while the social and natural sciences and the professional education core were placed solidly on this foundation. Quality rather than quantity was stressed with a plan that limited the number of courses and also demanded that each student be given study time for every class hour. Each student was to specialize in a particular area and further study was assured with a year of post-degree work. Finally the co-curricular program exposed the student to art, music, speech, literature, foreign languages, and physical education. The ideal had been set in place.

The value of the Everett Workshop was perhaps not so much in the plan it created but rather in the planning it spurred. Aside from questions that dealt with curriculum planning, the place of theology and philosophy, the importance of co-curriculars, the necessary training of teachers, the key question that Everett raised was: what kind of education should a sister be given and should it be better? Despite all the planning, thinking, researching, discussing, and consulting, the question was still not completely answered, nor could it be.

The never-ending search for the best way to prepare this special minister of the Church would continue. After the summer of 1956, however, the Sister Formation Conference could at least point to a published plan. This plan would generate new ideas, new college campus plans, new workshops--and most of all a new horizon for the American woman religious. Despite the needs of overcrowded classrooms, and hospitals and the demands of social works, "Sister Lucy" would get her education first. Despite the occasional misunderstandings of fellow sisters who knew only the "twenty year plan" of education, she would get a fully integrated and planned education. Despite the attitude of a male hierarchy that saw little need for women religious to study theology, she would be receiving a theological background. Respected as an individual, "Sister Lucy" was not only going to school but every aspect of her life was being recognized as important. She was to be holy and effective, psychologically mature, intellectually disciplined, broadly cultured and professionally competent.

CHAPTER IV   **GROWTH OF THE SISTER FORMATION CONFERENCE 1957-1960**

1957-1960 marked the next phase of activities for the Sister Formation Conference as it moved from the status of a temporary committee of the NCEA to that of a permanent section with the right to elect its own officers. 1954-1957 were years of initial growth noted particularly by the initiation of the regional conferences, the Everett Workshop, and continued research into the formation of American women religious. During this birthing period of the SFC, members concentrated on the educational needs of the American woman religious which had been sorely neglected. SFC participants brought these needs to light and recommended ways to meet them.

During 1957-1960 the conference experienced a deepening of its vision, goals, and challenges. Aware that personal growth had to be integrated to be complete, the SFC, led by Sister Mary Emil, saw the need to continue concentrating on the incorporation of apostolic growth with spiritual growth. In the mind of the SFC leadership, the well formed sister would be a successful sister.

> She will be a high-powered woman, in many ways at once. She must have deep spirituality, an intense prayer life issuing in a radiance of self-forgetting charity--and she must achieve this in spite of activity, work, distractions, and without long and uninterrupted hours of contemplations. She must be an informed, interesting, cultured person with a high degree of social ability--and this in spite of the demands on the one hand of her life of prayer and on the other of her professional duties. . . .There is something else--the Sister must have these qualities, and she must have them in an exquisite balance--a balance which doesn't come about by itself, but which will be the product of planning and training.[1]

The mobilizing and educating of American women religious was a long process, and the SFC recognized that the regional conferences, NCEA conventions, consultative visits, and published materials all helped to raise sisters to a new level of consciousness. Increasingly aware of the need for a complete education for the sister teacher, sister nurse, and sister social worker, religious communities were discussing more openly among themselves and with other communities the educational needs and standards to be met.

Providing each sister with a college degree before she entered her field of work full time appeared an awesome task. The Everett Curriculum was a major step in accomplishing this task. Another step remained: that of placing this educational experience into a proper context of formation. To accomplish this, the SFC sought to place attention on the juniorate experience in formation as the necessary partner of a liberal education. The apostolic constitution *Sedes Sapientiae* (1956), concerned with the formation of the male religious, would be applied analogously to the formation of sisters and would hasten interest in the juniorate movement as a way to integrate sister formation. The fleshing out of what a juniorate experience would mean for a sister in formation was a task from which the SFC did not shrink.

With the newly established secretariat of the SFC now set up at the NCEA headquarters in Washington, Sister Mary Emil was able to concentrate even more on setting direction for the conference. Aside from the six goals given priority as the conference entered its new phase as a section of the university and college department, the special concern of small communities was recognized. Challenging the university and college department of the NCEA to help these communities, Sister Mary Emil asked the assistance of those she knew could open doors for smaller religious communities that had neither a college nor a plan with another college.

> If we are to ask the sisterhoods to educate their members in regular sessions rather than summer schools, the arrangements must be set up whereby they can do so. . . .But we would like to leave with you the thought that it is the responsibility, if not in justice, then in charity, of the Sister Formation Committee, of this department, and of every college and university individually to see to it that, whenever a community in a given region feels ready to begin an adequate program of sister formation, it will not be prevented from doing so because of lack of facilities within a reasonable distance or under reasonable conditions.[2]

The help of educators, especially sister educators, continued to be vital in these next years as communities set up their educational systems.

At long range, sister formation in the small communities cannot succeed unless and until every college and university represented here assumes a positive responsibility toward the motherhouses and provincialates in its own district at least to discuss with the community officials what could be done.[3]

Sister Mary Emil continued by pleading that college officials consider the possibility of separate classes for sisters and a plan to train faculty members for sister colleges. It would be the continued work of the regional conferences and Marquette workshops to facilitate the work of this section with religious communities.

The Juniorate Theme in the Regional Conferences

The influence of the regional conferences was extended to the average sister in the religious community by means of the *Sister Formation Bulletin* and the publishing of the regional conference proceedings. For the first time, the ordinary sister was able to read and discuss that which was also read and discussed by the major superiors. Keenly aware of the impact of the regional conferences, the topics for the next conferences were again carefully selected. As Sister Mary Emil traveled to the regional conferences, she would visit religious communities to help with their individual problems.

We highly admired Sister Mary Emil because she seemed to have all the same objectives, philosophy and aims that we had in our own little college, and she was very humble; she was very active and she worked at this Sister Formation program until many of the colleges in the United States that were conducted for Sisters became members of the Sister Formation Conference.[4]

In 1956-57, the regional conferences had covered the topic of formation planning, and the Everett Curriculum had been the common ground for discussion. For the 1957-58 conferences, the Sister Formation Conference chose the juniorate as the focal point. The juniorate was seen as a new way of reaching personal integration. A period of not fewer than two years (yet not extending over the entire time of temporary vows), the juniorate was to be an exclusive time for spiritual and professional formation under the direction of a trained directress. It was to follow directly after the novitiate. A sister was a "junior" only when she participated in such a program. The juniorate program established for women in the formation process was not to be confused with a junior college program.

The Church had recommended the establishment of juniorates for women religious as early as 1952 but had left the implementation to each community. The SFC would forward that implementation by offering some common guidelines along with conference support. Sister Mary Emil wrote:

> We [sisters already out of formation] were products of a looser training, spiritually and academically. We will sacrifice for the new programs. We will probably not benefit from them personally. It is our high mission in this age of transition to see that a generation other than our own is trained to do the works we would like to have done but could not.[5]

Left to their own designs and ingenuity, women religious sought to model their programs after those of religious priests and brothers since these groups had documents to guide them. The apostolic constitution, *Sedes Sapientiae*, 31 May 1956, in which Pius XII dealt with the training of priests and religious men, was applied by Cardinal Arcadio Larraona, CMF, and Father Elio Gambari, SMM, as a model for the training of American women religious. The only viable indication of the Church's thinking concerning the proper formation of religious, this document stressed heavily the need for a definite period of post-novitiate time to be devoted to the spiritual, professional, and apostolic development of the person. The spiritual formation of the postulancy and the novitiate no longer seemed adequate. The added years of the juniorate would give the religious the time to steep himself/herself in the meaning of religious life. Professional demands required professional competence and this too would take time. The SFC desired to create a plan that would assure women religious of the special time needed to develop fully as a person. The usual obstacles, however, stood in the way of such assurance. The shortage of sisters was still a reason used by many to ignore the need for a juniorate period. Another reason given was that a sister once in habit could do anything, even without training. Lastly, it was feared that the sister allowed time in the juniorate would not have the proper community spirit.

To prepare for the regional meetings, major superiors were urged to read and study *Sedes Sapientiae*. This document occupied the attention of the regional participants. Also, Father Elio Gambari, of the Congregation for Religious, was asked to prepare a paper on the importance of the juniorate and this was to be read at each regional conference. With a background in canon law, he was seen as an expert on the workings of communities of women religious with special background in the foundation, development, rules and constitutions of women religious. Father Gambari made it clear to all that a juniorate was necessary, and his presentation became his introduction to sisters all over the United States and

Canada. Not only was his talk filled with new ideas and challenges, but it was also backed with the support of the Congregation for Religious. Father Gambari's name and work were soon commonly acknowledged by American women religious as he became more involved in religious formation in America.

Father Gambari based his presentation regarding the juniorate on a consideration of a "substantial and transforming new element--the apostolic vocation" in religious life.[6] This apostolic vocation was to take the sister from a cloistered atmosphere and give her a real share in the public role of the Church. She was to be not only a witness of prayerfulness and consecration but also dedicated to the ministry of charity. Certainly women religious were witnesses of charity in the apostolic works that they had done for years in America. Yet, "profound transformations have occurred in the environment in which religious women carry on their activity, with the result that the life of prayer, meditation, and seclusion from the world, necessary for spiritual progress and religious perfection has been made more difficult."[7] Sisters needed to recognize that they were not the only ones who served the needs of others. The state and other public institutions were now following their lead and sisters had to be equipped to meet professional demands. Apostolic demands of the day also would mean that sisters would have more contacts with others outside the religious community. This change would demand that the sister be able to carry the spirit of her rule flexibly into various situations. The master-apprentice system whereby a young sister was instructed in the ways of religious life and her professional duties was being replaced by organized educational programs. These educational programs, dictated by certification needs and curriculum plans such as Everett, demanded longer training periods for intellectual and professional growth. Finally, it was recognized that the young woman entering religious life may not have come from the same disciplined background her predecessors had. The preparation time needed to adapt to all these situations necessitated the inclusion of a juniorate program in the formation system of American women religious.

Father Gambari's message stimulated the use of new phrases in referring to sisters. "Public role," "Church's official mission," and "collaboration with the laity," were terms used that, when understood, would change the image and position of the sister from reactive to proactive.

In addition to the presentation by Father Gambari, each regional conference had a panel of representatives of various men's communities which had already implemented the aims of the juniorate in their communities. Opportunities were given the sisters for a question and answer period. Although the major superiors used this time as a chance to hear what was being done, they were not eager to simply imitate what the men had done. They recognized that "there are matters peculiar to the priests and others peculiar to the women" and therefore the education of sisters would be molded to the needs of a sister.[8]

The 1957-58 regional conferences sought to concentrate on the administration of the juniorate and the spiritual and intellectual formation in the juniorate. The published proceedings of these conferences, *The Juniorate in Sister Formation,* provided enough material to be a guide for a religious community wishing to establish a juniorate plan. A complete copy of Father Gambari's talk which had stirred so much action was published in this volume.

The SFC was able to engage Cardinal Larraona, backed with the authority of the Congregation for Religious, to write the forward for this volume and his section was to help allay the fears of those major superiors still hesitant about moving toward a comprehensive juniorate experience. Cardinal Larraona spoke of sisters in ministerial leadership and of the need for this role in the United States.

> The Juniorate has a major function to fulfill in the lives of our Sisters, especially in our days when the religious is called upon to exercise her apostolate in close association with, and in the name of, the church. It is especially in the United States that the Sisters complement, I might say, almost in an indispensable manner the ministry of the priest. It is especially for this reason that the Sister must be prepared for her mission with the utmost care in order to achieve the admirable unity of her life which will triumph in every crisis and which will testify to the world the prodigious efforts of which a soul is capable who has been privileged by God to enjoy a religious and apostolic vocation.[9]

The cardinal went on to point out the three categories that would determine the strength of a juniorate program: environment, administration, and the actual program for formation. Cardinal Larraona detailing the best environment further said: . . ."in the light of our knowledge of the psychology of young women it seems best that the Juniors should live in a section of the house either separate from the rest of the Community, or better still, in a house set aside only for the Juniorate. . . .It is of course clear that the atmosphere of study and professional formation will better achieve its aim if it is exclusively composed of religious."[10]

This situation was to allow for an atmosphere conducive for study and for professional and religious growth. The person to coordinate the juniorate experience was to be highly prepared for the work of spiritual and apostolic formation and exemplary in her own life. It was even suggested that the junior sisters come to live with several of these sisters so that a well-rounded formation would take place. The program recommended was to be highly formative, resting on the needs of the total person. The cardinal praised and held up programs like those already functioning at Providence Heights and at Marillac as ideals for other religious communities to imitate.

In speaking about the impact of the regional conferences based on the theme of the juniorate, Sister Mary Emil simply stated: "I think you will agree that the 1958 conferences have opened up a new phase of SF planning."[11] To which Sister Ritamary added:

> I think it is particularly wonderful news to know that they [the sisters] look to Sister Formation for help in drawing up that important legislation now in the offing for Sisters' training programs. It will be wonderful to see the Sisters' Sedes Sapientiae and to be able to look forward to a document that will stabilize some of the more important points stressed by the Sister Formation Conference, and I would almost take for granted, by much that is basic to Everett. Most of us would give blood for such a result. And soon.[12]

Although the first regional conferences were directed to pre-service formation, the concerns of 168,000 sisters already in the service of the church were also recognized by the SFC. These sisters, not having had the advantage of formation in a juniorate setting, were the working backbone of the Church's serving system, and the 1958-59 regional conferences focused on their needs. Topics covering the psychological, professional and spiritual aspects of inservice formation were presented. A research project was conducted to obtain source materials for the regional conferences. Questionnaires were sent to 10,000 teaching sisters and one hundred seventy-three major superiors by Sister Elizabeth Ann, IHM. The continued study patterns for these in-service sisters in every community was the focal issue. To approach the problem in an organized manner was most critical, and each community was encouraged to study the needs of their sisters already working full-time and then to proceed with a plan for future action. The challenge of formation seemed never ending as major superiors began to realize that every sister needed some type of continued formation. One regional group advocated religious conferences, reading circles, discussion groups, guided reading, and opportunities for advanced college and university work for the in-service sister. Sister Mary Emil presented a talk entitled "The Local Superiors--In-Service Agent of Sister Formation" as she travelled from one regional group to another. Workshops, conferences, and study plans sprang up all over the country and, publicized in the Sister Formation Bulletin, became patterns for sisters all over the United States. These regional conferences stimulated action in communities, making the concerns of the in-service sister better known.

In the fall of 1959, the leadership conference of the SFC moved that there would be no formal regional conferences for 1959-60 in order to prepare better for regional conferences on the topic of the juniorate in 1960-61. It was agreed that a study should be made concerning information on present juniorates as source material for the conferences. Furthermore, it was decided that two planning meetings would take place in the regions in order to organize possible visits to existing juniorates. This study would be one among many that the SFC would sponsor to help in the establishment of the juniorate.

NCEA Conventions

The convening of the Sister Formation Section at the 1958 NCEA convention marked the first time it was meeting with a section status, a privilege given the SFC at the 1957 NCEA convention. This meant that no committee report was necessary. Admission was again by ticket only. Following up on a theme that had already been considered as early as 1956 when two national studies had been done, one on the attitude of high school and college girls toward religious vocations (Sister Judith) and the other on the inservice needs of teaching sisters (Sister Elizabeth Ann), the 1958 conference considered the use of time in formation from the aspect of the sister teacher and the sister student. It was determined that the sister student in the juniorate would have the following time schedule: 3-4 hours-prayer, 1-1/2 hours-meals, 7-7 1/2 hours-sleep, 1/2 hour-household duties, 1 hour-recreation, 1/2 hour-necessary 'self-preservation', 1 hour-self-transportation (going to bed; getting up) and 8 hours for class and study. This would mean that for every hour of class, there would be an hour and twenty-two minutes of study (considering the sister took fourteen to sixteen hours of college work).[13] The sister in formation experienced a strict structuring of her study and personal time. The fact that her schedule was being considered in order to allow for proper study time was an indication of a growing concern for the needs of the individual person. This theme fit in well with the simultaneous study going on within the regional meetings on the topic of the in-service sister. In order to understand the position and attitudes of various groups, a major superior, school superintendent, pastor, directress of studies, local superior, and teacher were asked to present papers on this topic within their own area of competency.

The issue of time was addressed in several ways and all of them in a practical sense. Immediately considered was the daily schedule of the sister. Communities began to discuss and experiment with ways to increase study time by re-arranging and changing the schedule of the sister student. Shortened or private prayer times, unstructured recreation, and reduced cleaning schedules were ways to center a little more attention on the academic needs of the sister. Even the amount of care and time devoted to the religious habit were discussed when looking for ways to gain study time. Sisters were beginning to question whether time spent on making, mending, and caring for elaborate habits was absolutely necessary. Unscheduled time for individual needs and enjoyment was not yet part of the sister's schedule for that aspect of personal growth was still to be explored.

Attitudes were beginning to change. Sisters could no longer be considered twenty-four hour ministers with no time for refueling or professional growth. Time needed to be allotted for professional growth. Several ways were suggested to help gain time for the in-service sister. Engaging more lay teachers and working with them in a cooperative manner was suggested as a necessary step to meet the demands of quality education and to secure more time for sisters to continue their education. Re-doing the school calendar and vacation times to accommodate periods for study and necessary rest rather than for house cleaning were offered as a more efficient use of professional time. These suggestions were offered for two reasons: "to free the Sister so that she can do the teaching she is appointed to do, and use the talents and professional training she has brought to the school . . . to give the Sisters more time and more opportunities to develop and grow in their professional character while in service."[14]

Another concern voiced at this convention was that of finances. Communities were being asked to put up new buildings and establish new educational programs for the beginning sister along with financing the continued education of the sister active in the apostolate. Seeking ways to fund the future education of sisters would be the impetus behind another activity of the SFC.

Since the NCEA convention was a key opportunity to gather together religious communities from all over the nation, it is not surprising that the 1959 NCEA session for the SFC concentrated on a increasingly vital question: that of personnel policies for the sister colleges. There was a concern about the quality of faculty, a concern that had also surfaced during the Marquette workshops. A proposed personnel policy for faculty of sister colleges contained recommendations that a sister be trained to the Ph.D. level if she was to serve on a college staff. That she be informed early in her career of the possibility of an administrative or college faculty position was also required so that she could take full advantage of educational opportunities and also have a time of apprenticeship. It was highly recommended that an inservice plan be put in writing for every college teacher and administrator, lay or religious, and that this should include among other avenues of enrichment, the use of every third summer as a refresher or study summer. A more practical suggestion that was made was freeing the college teacher of general household duties so that the time could be used for study, writing, and research. The conclusion to these proposals indicated the advantages sought:

1. It [everything proposed above] would encourage all of us to discard expediency and insist on what we know to be better--total vision, long-range planning.
2. It would encourage our sister faculties to become great scholars and win many scholar-saints for the Church.
3. It would maintain for all of us concerned with college faculties and accrediting agencies the status which we now possess; it would gain for us the confidence of our sister faculty members that we really do want an intellectual climate on our campus, and it would convince everyone that it is possible to have intellectual giants in every classroom.[15]

A second session at this same NCEA convention was limited to major superiors and one member appointed by each major superior. Communities which had no colleges of their own or had not established a cooperative plan with another college were especially encouraged to attend. Representatives of communities that had women's colleges and wished to help with the problem of organizing and receiving accreditation for small sisters' colleges were welcomed. Once again, the SFC made it clear that it was up to each community to decide what form of educational program was needed. The options extended to establishing one's own college, becoming an institutional branch of another college, or sending sisters to a college of another community. No option was given to remain without any plan, so all communities were expected to establish some kind of arrangement.

In order to facilitate a profitable and orderly session, participants were asked to send in questions before the convention began. A panel was assembled to address these questions. The audience was encouraged to participate and though only half of the questions were thoroughly covered, it was the general consensus of the group that it was a good beginning and that the unanswered questions should be addressed at another time. The questions covered every aspect of sister education: the weak and strong points of a small sisters' college; how to organize such a college; how to determine faculty salaries. The interest in this topic would continue to grow and to occupy the time and energy of the SFC activities.

The sessions of the 1960 NCEA convention again addressed the issue of personnel policies for sister college teachers. Participants resumed discussions from the previous year and felt that the most important point of the policies was that which designated that twenty percent of each class should go on for higher education and then to positions in the community that would profit from such an education, i.e., formation, administration, college faculties. A strong spokesperson for this point was Sister Madeleva, who at a previous NCEA convention (1949) had introduced the educational concerns of "Sister Lucy" to all. Now she was pleading that "Sister Lucy" should go on to graduate school.

The participants also dealt with the organization and accreditation of sister colleges. Using the previous year's plan, questions about these colleges were submitted and discussed. From the one hundred forty-seven participants, forty-nine separate problems were raised. So much interest was present that an evening session was scheduled for those who could stay longer. The interest in this topic underscored the fact that many communities were struggling with questions about affiliation, curriculum, physical facilities, and financing. It was one thing to have the Everett Curriculum, but every community faced the practical questions of how to put the curriculum into practice, how to educate sisters to the doctoral level in order to become the faculty for the ideal sister college, and how to secure the necessary state approval for accreditation. To complicate the issue, all of these plans had financial implications and the stipends which teaching sisters earned as salaries did not take into account that education was costly.

Sister Colleges

The revamping of educational practices among American religious women in the mid-and-late 1950s represented more changes than any casual observer could note. The rising juniorate buildings on or near college campuses were the response of women religious to a triple plea: the Catholic Church's calling for professionally prepared ministers, the state accrediting agencies' promoting proper credentialing, and the religious communities' seeking to prepare their sisters in a complete and human manner. The sister college was the brick and mortar response to this call. The education received rested on the foundation of the Everett model of a liberal arts education and the juniorate model of integrated spiritual, intellectual and professional growth.

The sister college was meant to provide an undergraduate education for sisters while they were in formation. The thinking behind the sister college was that the confines of a religious community setting would provide a more fruitful atmosphere for integrative learning. Though the co-ed university could offer the sister the opportunity of a varied faculty, fine library and laboratory facilities, and the experience of mixing with male and female, lay and religious co-students, it was generally felt by major superiors that this educational experience should be reserved for graduate work when, in effect, the sister would be more mature. Unspoken was the belief that without a solid undergraduate foundation the sister would not be ready for the challenges of graduate work in a secular environment.

The undergraduate study of the sister in a sister college was to give her a solid education steeped in a religious formation that would prepare her for a work in the Church. Her undergraduate study was to be protected against unnecessary distraction. Her special undergraduate education was to allow for co-curricular activities and leadership opportunities not afforded a sister at a regular college or university.

The sister college was successful at keeping the sister from the distractions of the world, but it was not at all clear how successful it was in preparing the sister for the work of ministry in the world. Experiencing education in a semi-cloistered atmosphere did not allow for the integrative learning that the SFC sought to promote. For many smaller communities, however, the sister college was the best tool they could use to bring their sisters into an educational setting. Communities that owned and operated their own colleges had two options: to allow their sisters to study side by side with the lay women or to build a juniorate on their own campus and establish a special atmosphere for their sisters. Though the Church recommended the latter situation, communities were free to chose what they would do. The smaller communities without their own previously established college had the hardest decision to make. Hoping that these communities would seek out already established facilities of other religious communities, the SFC sought to link communities together for this purpose. Marillac College, owned and operated by the Daughters of Charity in St. Louis, was an example of a college that opened its doors to many religious communities. Providence Heights College was an example of a "college within a college," operating as a branch college of Seattle University. The College of Saint Teresa was established as a lay woman's college and there lay and religious went to school together.

A remaining option for a religious community was to organize its own college. When a religious community was large enough and had enough sisters and finances to train a faculty and provide adequate facilities, this option was viable. However, enthusiasm and zeal were not enough. Not all communities were able to have their own colleges and still maintain high quality. The biggest reasons for this were small numbers in the student body, partially prepared faculty, and high expenses. The basis for this concern rested on the fact that by 1960 there were ninety-three sister colleges (forty-nine had come into existence since 1950) with enrollments of fewer than fifty-five students and with sixty-nine percent of the faculties with only an M.A. or less.

There were many problems connected with the proliferation of these small sister colleges. Concern over the small motherhouse colleges that were quickly springing up was shared by the SFC, the College and University Department of the NCEA, and by accrediting agencies. At this time, only three motherhouse colleges had received accreditation: Providence Heights, Notre Dame (St.

Louis), and Marillac. Chief concerns of the accrediting agencies for the other colleges included facilities that were too limited to create an academic atmosphere, faculty size that would not allow for an adequate intellectual climate, and isolation that promoted insular thinking and inbreeding. Finally, the financial resources needed for establishing and maintaining such educational facilities would tax even the larger of the communities. Maintaining quality education had to be done in a realistic manner, and fine dreams could not always be easily financed.

Early discussions concerning a proper environment for sister education dealt with the question of whether this educational environment should be isolated or integrated. It was the strong view of Sister Mary Emil that sisters should be educated differently from their lay peers, and this was supported by the stated desire of the Church, even if it meant that the religious community begin its own college to attain this end. Not everyone was in agreement with this opinion. Sister Emmanuel from the College of Saint Teresa explained that she and Sister Mary Emil agreed to disagree on this topic. Thus, the sisters attending the College of Saint Teresa--while following the Everett Curriculum--attended some of their classes with lay people. "She [Sister Mary Emil] really thought there was a difference. . . .She really felt that they shouldn't be contaminated by the presence of the lay people. I don't believe that, I think a young sister needs to be relating."[16] Sister Josetta Butler, RSM, pointed out:

> From the very beginning, Sister Emil and I, disagreed with the premise that the education of our young sisters should be conducted in an atmosphere of complete isolation from any secular contacts. The student body would be made up of only sisters and the faculty likewise would be comprised of only religious teachers. Marillac College and Providence Heights College were established on this premise. I believed it was important that the young sisters be able to compete with the lay students in our Catholic Women's Colleges and benefit from the presence of lay professors as well as religious teachers.[17]

Despite opposition, SFC leadership would continue to promote separate sister education as the better way since it was the desire of the Church. It was the larger communities that Sister Mary Emil feared would discourage the separate education issue even though pronouncements had been made from the Congregation for Religious. The experience of these communities with established colleges for lay women, colleges that their own sisters attended, had given them a different and wider vision of how sister education should be handled.

Another aspect of sister education, the in-service of sister faculty members for these sister colleges, was to be the prime reason for summer workshops that would come to be known as the Marquette Workshops. With emphasis on the preparation of the faculty involved in sister education, the study of the Everett Curriculum was the focal issue. These workshops sought to work with sister faculty members in order to bring about a better understanding of the kind of education needed for the sister of tomorrow.

Marquette Workshops

The Marquette Workshops were designed to study the Everett Curriculum and to help the faculty plan and develop programs to put it in place. In the 1957 winter issue of the Sister Formation Bulletin, the first Marquette Workshop was announced. Spearheaded by SFC leadership, which had discussed the workshops at its leadership meeting that fall, and guided by Dr. John Riedl of Marquette University, the early plans envisioned the Marquette Workshops as providing an opportunity for further study and evaluation of the Everett Curriculum. It was Sister Mary Emil's hope that Marquette would sponsor the project. "The project could be well initiated, I think, by a letter from the University announcing the proposed workshop, saying that the registration would be limited (which always gets them), and perhaps asking for an expression of opinion on whether they would care to have graduate credit or not. I think it could be determined from the type of person who signs up whether it should be a straight presentation of the Everett material, or a critical evaluation plus a constructive effort to improve upon the Everett proposals."[18]

Under the direction of Sister Elizabeth Ann, IHM, and sponsored by Marquette University, the workshop was to explore further the applications of the Everett Curriculum to the individual formation programs of religious communities. Directresses of study and the administration and faculty of juniorates were advised to attend and could either audit the session or receive three hours of graduate credit. Five sister experts in education were selected as discussion leaders and resource people for the three-week session. The first workshop held in August of 1958 was attended by over one hundred sisters from all over the United States representing thirty-seven different religious communities with a total membership of 60,000. In order to achieve a basic goal of sharing between communities, discussion groups, general meetings, question periods and round-table groups were arranged so that each religious community was represented. There was a special emphasis on the place of liberal education in the complete educational schema of the sister. At one point it was hoped that the workshop, if successful at Marquette, would then be repeated in different parts of the country and at different colleges. This never happened--perhaps because the regional conferences in the 1960s sponsored meetings for communities to meet with the colleges in each region for more personal planning.

In the invitational letter to sisters for the first workshop, Sister Elizabeth Ann indicated that the purpose of the Marquette Workshop was not to create a pattern for a good college education but rather "to set up guidelines for the collegiate education of Sisters which would be focused upon the Sister not only as a person, but also as a religious dedicated to the service of God."[19] The plea again was to investigate the integration of the spiritual and the intellectual in order to provide for more effective apostolic work. The curriculum "must provide a true liberal arts education directed toward a disinterested love of truth and the development of the Sister as a person, but within and through that education it must enkindle, also, a tremendous love for the apostolate."[20] This workshop was to offer an opportunity for sister faculty to work on practical applications of the Everett curriculum. The sisters were to learn that it was not enough to be well prepared in their fields. They had to have an understanding of the whole framework of the curriculum.

The task of assimilating the thinking behind the Everett Curriculum and the recommendations was a big task even for a well organized three-week span. The two demonstration centers for the curriculum, Providence Heights and the College of Saint Teresa, were still in the implementation stages on their campuses, yet their input was considered very important at this workshop. Aside from providing inservice to college faculty and community education directresses, this workshop allowed for inter-community discussions and planning.

Sisters returned home after this workshop and began to spread what they had learned. Copies of the talks were circulated, local college curriculums were studied against the Everett Curriculum and Marquette guidelines, and local discussion groups were established to talk about and plan for pre-service and in-service training of their sisters.

Due to the positive response after the first workshop, a second workshop was scheduled for the following summer. Once again the Everett Curriculum was examined with an emphasis on meeting individual community needs. There were opportunities to fine-tune the already existing Everett curriculum schema. "I think the role of the Marquette Workshops was in correcting what I felt were over-concentrations, let us say, and giving it directions and leading it certainly into the wider aspect of many disciplines,"[21] remarked Sister Ritamary Bradley. Discussion of what was important and changing in sister education allowed the emphasis of the Marquette Workshops to change dramatically in the next years.

Father Gambari, who was becoming a trusted guide to the SFC and American women religious, also taught Marquette participants beginning with this second workshop. Perhaps only someone who attended all SFC sponsored conferences and workshops could see how all the activities led to one goal--that of better understanding the changing face of religious life and thus the need to change formation programs. The sharing of Father Gambari's thoughts on the juniorate, if only by means of tape recordings at this session, was another way to help the sisters present to examine the correlation of the spiritual with the intellectual.

The Marquette Workshops, however, did not attract the same sisters each year so there was no way to build from one year to the other. In 1959, sixty sisters representing twenty-five communities (20,000 sisters) participated, most of whom had not attended the previous year. The NCEA conventions and the regional conferences along with the quarterly publication of the Sister Formation Bulletin helped to fill in the gaps.

The 1960 Marquette Workshop on the theme of "The Role of the Faculty in Sister Formation" correlated appropriately with like themes in other SFC activities. This workshop, again studying the Everett Curriculum, put a special emphasis on the faculty's role of planning and implementing the courses of study within a total juniorate structure. The opening address by Father Gambari provided the backbone idea for the workshop, namely, cooperative team work by the college faculty and formation directresses as one of the keys to the integration of the intellectual with the spiritual. Educating sisters, whether from the standpoint of the intellectual or the spiritual, was seen as an extraordinary task; but, without a team approach, the whole process of juniorate formation was viewed as departmentalized and not effective.

> It is a very different thing to teach Sisters than to teach lay women, for in the formation of Sisters the instructors must show themselves essentially Christ-like. . . .Lay women can say: We are not called to the state of perfection; we are not expected to be so mortified. But when the students are Sisters, there is the opportunity to form Christ in them in a perfect way.[22]

References used for the workshop included the Everett Report, the SFC proceedings on the juniorate, past editions of the Sister Formation Bulletin, and *Sedes Sapientiae*. A great deal of time was spent going over these documents with the view of seeing how each person on the formation team had a role to play.

The superior, chaplain, directress of studies, formation directress, and the teachers were to operate as a team so that all aspects of education were integrated. "Faculty" was defined as anyone who worked with sister-students. This sister formation faculty was expected to construct and administer curriculum, to establish a community atmosphere on the sister college campus, and to help the sister student integrate her learning experiences. The others were to work hand in hand, even to the point of teaching some of the classes in order to better understand what was being taught, and of helping to make the complete juniorate schedule a learning experience. It was noted that the juniorate directress was key to the whole operation, particularly when it came to supplementing the learning in the classroom with times of spiritual instruction, times of relaxation, and times of cultural experiences.

Policy statements dealing with the implementation of the curriculum for sisters by religious faculty were recommended to communities as a result of this workshop. The growing concern that real integrative learning could not take place without a cooperative and open religious formation atmosphere was stressed. Even if the educational norms were set, they could not be fully implemented until initial formation caught up with those norms. Practical examples of this were the need of the sister student to consult the faculty member after school hours even if there was rule of silence, and the time they needed to study, time that sometimes had to be taken away from community activities. Cooperation and understanding were the key if this type of sister formation was to be a team effort. The serious concern of the participants to make sister formation a priority can be seen in these selected norms, each of which may have been counter to previous religious customs:

1. The most important work of a religious community is the formation of its members.
2. What is best for the Sisters' formation will take precedence over every other consideration.
3. For the Sister who has been assigned to academic work, study is her major apostolic activity.
4. Serious consideration should be given to having some of the faculty members share in the community life of the Sisters in the juniorate.[23]

If the Marquette Workshops did nothing else but allow for candid discussions of the sister curriculum according to these new norms, they fulfilled a great need. This was a time of learning new ways and learning them quickly. These workshops also demonstrated that the SFC was helping to build up a strong cadre of sisters that would better understand what was to happen in the quickly rising juniorate buildings.

To strengthen the organized effort of the SFC to present a new plan for the formation of the sister, yet another series of programs was introduced. The Instructional Programs in Spirituality (IPS) were to concentrate on the spiritual aspects of formation. Though every activity of the SFC stressed a different aspect of formation, i.e., Marquette Workshops, the academic, the Instructional

Programs,   and the spiritual, time was always taken to stress the need for integration of the intellectual and the spiritual.

Instructional Programs in Spirituality

Looked upon as a great advance for sister formation, the instructional programs in spirituality were born out of a desire to set up a program in spirituality that would harmonize with a sister's intellectual formation. The SFC chose Father Elio Gambari, SMM, of the Congregation for Religious, as the main instructor in this program. Father Gambari, whose paper on the juniorate had been so favorably received, was asked to prepare and deliver a series of conferences that would outline a five-year program of spiritual instruction paralleling the Everett course of studies. In 1959, under the direction of the SFC, Father Gambari directed the first workshops. With the purpose of pulling together the spiritual, intellectual, professional, and apostolic points of formation within the context of each individual community, these sessions/workshops were held at the College of Sister Formation, Seattle University, and the College of Saint Teresa, Winona, Minnesota. The workshops were set up specifically for directresses of postulants, novices and junior sisters and lasted a full week. A five-year plan of spiritual instruction, entitled "Syllabus of Spiritual Instructions" was presented. This was a program of spiritual instruction for the young religious as she moved through the stages of formation of postulancy, novitiate, and juniorate. Practical means of discussion, study, exposure to new ideas in theology, and an opportunity to mingle with other communities were provided at each conference. By means of several lectures and a question period each day, the participants were exposed to concerns of the spiritual life. Comments told of the success of these workshops: "This workshop marks a new development within sister formation, one which will be responsible for a re-evaluation of our techniques for perfecting the spiritual life of our young sisters."[24]   This was pointed out in these comments of Cardinal Valeri, prefect of the Sacred Congregation of Religious:

> With you, I, too, am convinced that the enlightened effort that is being made by the Sister Formation Conferences to deepen and systematize the spiritual training of the young Religious of the United States will have significant and lasting consequences. For from Workshops such as your Conferences have been promoting, the mistresses of postulants and novices and junior professed Sisters will be able to draw solid principles which will save them from so much needless floundering in forming themselves for their important tasks. Father Gambari is particularly well equipped and

qualified for the direction and assistance that he has been giving to the Conferences, because of his interest and experience in this field. We are happy to hear the favorable comments that have been made about his contribution.[25]

The popularity of Father Gambari was in part due to the fact that he was seen as a representative from Rome, voicing the wishes of the Church. The amount of material that he presented gave all who attended something to work with. His interpretation of spirituality was fresh and widened the definition of religious life to include a more active apostolic life. "The religious life of Sisters engaged in teaching, in aiding the sick, or in other ministries represents a vocation of the religious woman that is new in the Church. Such a vocation, while it preserves all the content of perfection and sanctity transmitted to us by traditional religious life and intensified through the centuries, has been enriched by a substantial element. This enrichment profoundly affects the traditional element. Indeed, it transforms it. This new element is the call to a direct and immediate apostolate to the good of our neighbor in the forms which best suit the nature and potentialities of a woman. We have thus a religious-apostolic vocation."[26]

Because of the high level of success of the first workshops in Instructional Programs in Spirituality and because many sisters had been unable to attend the first ones, Father Gambari conducted two workshops on spirituality in the summer of 1960. He reworked and expanded on the previous year's materials after consulting with the SFC leadership, and this time each workshop lasted three weeks.

Father Gambari would arrange his summer schedule in such a way that he was able to do these workshops and also be present for other SFC activities, particularly the Marquette Workshops and the SFC leadership meetings. This allowed for extended input and guidance. Ample correspondence indicates that this "little Italian" soon became a confidant of the SFC and of many individuals connected with the movement.

Relationship of the Conference of Major Superiors with the Sister Formation Conference

Important to the operations of the SFC during this time was the relationship of the newly founded organization of the Conference of Major Superiors of Women, the CMSW, with the SFC. Having always been aware of the position and power of the major superior and having in the early years of the SFC always included her in their activities, the SFC had now to learn how to work with an organization that united this special group of religious. The question at hand was how the SFC would continue to operate under the authority of the Conference of

Major Religious Superiors of Women's Institutes, and within the framework of the NCEA. The SFC did not want to come under the direct authority of the CMSW for they had experienced an autonomy under the NCEA that they did not wish to lose. This desire for free and independent action later became a point of strong disagreement between the SFC and the CMSW.

The struggle to stay free of the CMSW would be difficult and in the end would not succeed. In 1957, the SFC had received news which made the SFC believe they were free of the CMSW. It dealt with the procedure the conference was to use in requesting permission for its meetings. Cardinal Larraona, CMF, secretary of the Congregation for Religious, in a letter written to Father Paul C. Reinert, SJ, president of the College and University Department of the NCEA, stated that the CMSW would be establishing a committee on formation but that the SFC would continue to function under the authority of the NCEA.

> It is evident that the complete formation, spiritual, intellectual, technical, etc., of the young Religious and the integration of all the elements of that formation for whatever special activity the Sisters will exercise, are primarily and fundamentally the responsibility of the Major Superiors. But these in turn need and welcome advice and assistance of experts in their quest for the surest and best adapted means to attain the end they must accomplish. Here, we feel, the Sister Formation Conferences have an important role to play, especially in the field of education, through their affiliation with the National Catholic Education Association.[27]

A later letter written by Cardinal Larraona to Mother Alcuin, OSF, national chairperson of the CMSW, however, caused some concern because it appeared to indicate that an even closer relationship between the two groups was desired by the Congregation for Religious. It had been true that the SFC had handled weighty matters of formation long before the creation of the CMSW, but the Congregation for Religious wanted to make it perfectly clear that the formation of the sisters was the primary responsibility of every major superior. The SFC, it was felt, could remain within the NCEA to help with the practical issues of intellectual formation only.

> With specific reference to the Sister Formation Conferences, which have been doing such excellent work during the past several years . . . They are therefore to be under the direction and control of the Conference of Major Superiors, and the action of the Conference in their regard is to be reported to this Sacred

Congregation [of religious] in its regular communications to the Holy See.[28]

The words "under the direction and control of the Conference of Major Superiors," left the SFC with little room for independent action. It was as if clear lines had been set up to delineate that spiritual formation was under the religious superiors and the intellectual formation in the hands of the SFC. In many respects, this division militated against growth in thinking among women religious. Part of the thrust of the SFC was to allow all to have responsibility in the formation process. This action departmentalized areas of authority and spoke a clear message that superiors had certain rights no other sisters could have.

Due to this new directive, the executive committees of both the SFC and the CMSW met with two representatives from the Congregation for Religious, Father Bernard Ransing, CSC, and Father Elio Gambari, in August of 1958, to delineate lines of authority. It was decided that a committee composed of three major superiors appointed by the CMSW would meet with and act as a liaison with the national chairperson and executive secretary of the SFC. This CMSW committee joined the SF leadership group as voting members.

> The control and direction of the Sister Formation Conference by the Higher Superiors Conference will be exercised through the attendance by these three Mothers at all Sister Formation leadership meetings, where they will have veto power on any decision on which they are in agreement[sic]. They will report in writing to the Executive Committee of the Higher Superiors Conference on their exercise of such control over SFC, and this report will be incorporated into the account submitted annually to the Sacred Congregation of Religious.[29]

It was also determined that permission for all SF meetings would now go to the Congregation for Religious through the CMSW rather than the NCEA. Father Ransing and Father Elio Gambari explained that the CMSW was viewed as a "vertical organization" whose goal was to oversee the whole of religious life and its activities, including education, vocation, and formation. The SFC was identified as a specialized or "horizontal organization" that the CMSW formation committee, composed only of major superiors, could go to for advice. Policy decisions regarding the formation of sisters were, however, in the hands of the CMSW.

Even though coming under the authority of the CMSW was an action that the SFC had not desired, the leadership of the SFC stated its loyalty to the CMSW, equating this loyalty to obedience to the wishes of the Church. Sr. Mary Emil wrote:

> I would like also to take this opportunity, Mother, to assure you that we understand and are happy over the desire of the Sacred Congregation for Religious that the Sister Formation Conferences work under the control and direction of the Major Religious Superiors Conference. It was very encouraging to have Father Gambari and Father Ransing at our Leadership Meeting in South Bend to explain the spirit and the manner in which we should try to carry this out. The Fathers pointed out that not everything could be settled at once because both organizations were in evolution and we understand the need for a gradual working out of arrangements. Nevertheless, I want you to know, Mother, that this office is completely at your service.[30]

Sister Mary Emil was concerned, though, that the major superiors would just not understand the goals and direction of the SFC and in a later letter wrote, "They [major superiors] don't know enough about our organization to be able to give the kind of background, answers, and explanations that would be requested."[31] This constant concern about how the SFC would function if totally under the CMSW runs like an unbroken thread through this part of the history.

For a presentation to the American bishops in 1959, Sister Mary Emil composed the "Memorandum on Sister Formation Conference" that was delivered by Msgr. Hochwalt, the director of the NCEA. This memorandum contained reasons why it was best that the SFC stay under the operational authority of the NCEA.

> It is believed that the continued operation of the Sister Formation Conference within the Association can be advantageous both to the Conference of Major Superiors and to the National Catholic Educational Association. The religious superiors will have the advantage of the National Catholic Educational Association's access to information and professional contacts; the Association in turn, through the College and University Department, will be able to exert an influence on the education of sisters which will provide better teachers for the schools and an almost certain increase in religious vocations. To date, no conflict in the jurisdiction of the two organizations has arisen. The N.C.E.A. assumes financial responsibility for the national secretariat; the religious communities, by their donations and lecture stipends, finance the

travel and general expenses of the conference and its officers. . .
Although the finances of the Conference are precarious, and
although the dual authorization may present insuperable
complications in the future, of a kind which would suggest that the
Major Superiors' Conference take over the work entirely, it is felt
that the present arrangement is satisfactory. Sister Formation at
the N.C.E.A. can be sensitive to the needs of the hospitals and
schools, and to the apostolate of the Church in the United States,
in a way which might not be possible otherwise.[32]

With the establishment of the liaison committee and a promise from both
organizations to work together, the situation seemed workable. As long, too, as
the SFC could work directly under the NCEA, another aspect of the SFC was
saved and that was its ability to act as a non-canonical group.

Sister Emil, in good faith, felt that the program would never reach
its goals if the SFC was placed under the CMSW. She wanted the
program to be able to develop free from the canonical control of
superiors. She knew the pressures from pastors on these superiors
to staff the increasing number of new elementary schools as well
as the demands to supply high school teachers for the secondary
schools now being established, would be a tremendous obstacle.
To meet these demands could only result in the continued
assignment of untrained teachers. The vision needed to foresee the
future demands for educated sister-teachers was not there![33]

In a confidential memo to Mother Mary Consolatrice, BVM, the head of the
CMSW executive committee, Sister Mary Emil made suggestions as to areas that
the two organizations could work on together. These included investigating
health services for communities acting cooperatively, watching legislation which
might affect educational opportunities for sisters, publishing a CMSW newsletter
for major superiors, helping to place vocation work into the hands of sisters and
not priests, and representing CMSW at meetings of other organizations.

Though not necessary, approval was sought of the new SFC executive
secretary from the CMSW by Sister Mary Emil. Politically aware, she advised
that "it might carry more weight with the major superior who is approached for
a sister to fulfill this office if the request is presented by the Major Superiors
Executive Committee after the person had been selected by the formation
leadership group."[34]   Much concern surrounded the position of executive
secretary of the SFC and lobbying began early for Sister Mary Emil's successor.
Sister Annette Walters, CSJ, was the one selected. Sister Annette took office on

1 September 1960. Sister Mary Emil was happy with Sister Annette's selection; for she had personally groomed her as her successor.

> Far from representing any break in the continuity of our effort, this change, we truly feel, can mean an enhancement and a solidifying of every good for which the movement has stood, so that in ten years from now we will look back upon this time as representing a step up to a distinctly higher level of activity.[35]

To insure a way of communicating with higher superiors, the SFC began to publish the Sister Formation Newsletter for Higher Superiors in December 1957. The purpose of this publication was to keep major superiors aware of current happenings, issues, and to provide information on grants, scholarships and fellowships for sister students as quickly as possible. This publication was strictly for the major superior while the circulation of the Sister Formation Bulletin was still for all sisters.

These first years of co-existence between the SFC and the CMSW were marked with uncertainty and caution, due largely to the hazy delineation of how they were to work together. The area of formation, set down clearly by Church law as a responsibility of the major superiors, had for four years previous to the founding of the CMSW, been in the hands of the SFC. The question now before the major superiors was what to do with the SFC. Should it be brought totally under the CMSW? Should it be allowed to go on but with supervision and constant approval? The fact that the Congregation for Religious had already spoken highly of the work of the SFC and had looked with approval on its connection with the NCEA steered the CMSW in the direction of deciding that a liaison committee would be sufficient for the time being. It appears that the major superiors knew that at this time it would not have been a good political move to put the SFC directly under its authority. No one could deny the good work that had been accomplished by the SFC; the CMSW saw itself now as a controller and guide of that good work. The charismatic leadership of a grass-roots group of women, the SFC, now had to learn how to deal with the appointed leadership of an institutional organization of women, the CMSW.

Conclusion

New times were giving American women religious new challenges, and in an organized and systematic manner, sisters attempted to update educational and formational systems within a decade. The call of the Church had been given, the need for updating credentials was felt, and all sisters went into action, some hesitantly and some in the vanguard. It was the SFC that provided avenues to research data that could be used for decision making and future planning. The regional meetings offered opportunities for communities to share, discuss, and build together. The published materials of the SFC gave communities and individual members access to first hand theological trends and information. The SFC was an educational tool well used and expanding in its scope.

To the CMSW, the SFC provided not only an example of organization and sharing but also a challenge. The SFC, born out of the educational needs of American sisters and fashioned by a group of sisters already in higher education, struggled with its changing role as the CMSW, created by a desire of the Congregation for Religious to have women's communities plan and work together in America, assumed an umbrella responsibility for every aspect of sister life.

American religious had begun to ask some serious questions about themselves and take some serious actions in the 1950s. In ten years, sisters had won the right to be educationally qualified before beginning their ministry. Sisters themselves questioned their conventual life style. Schedule, habit, and customs were being examined in the light of service to the Church in a modern age. "Sister Lucy" was entering a new age, and the SFC continued to struggle with the questions of how to best educate this sister.

CHAPTER V   TIME OF TRANSFORMATION   1960-1964

If Sister Lucy were to continue to receive an integrated education, much work still remained to be done. It was not enough that the SFC had orchestrated workshops and conferences, publications, and consultative opportunities. There remained yet the work of helping this to happen for all communities. Identifying with American women religious and their causes, the SFC continued to struggle to bring to light the needs of the sisters. Between 1954 and 1960, the Sister Formation Conference had grown in strength of purpose and had moved into new areas of activity. More significant changes took place in the years 1960-1964. The SFC continued to spread its influence in the United States and then beyond the borders of the United States with its sister formation activities. The leadership of the SFC fell to Sister Annette Walters, CSJ, in 1960 and Sister Mary Emil remained a part of the SFC leadership for another year on a consulting basis. In September 1961, Sister Mary Emil was called to assume the presidency of Marygrove College in Detroit. Sister Ritamary Bradley, CHM, joined Sister Annette as her assistant in 1961, and the two worked as a team until 1964 when new leadership was put in place. Vatican Council II began in 1962, and a sister, Mary Luke Tobin, SL, was asked to come as an observer. By August of 1964, the SFC was named a committee of the CMSW. All of these events were significant to the SFC. Entering its second generation of growth with new leadership, new ideas, and new demands, the SFC would change from an organization with its eyes on the total educational needs of the pre-service sister to an organization settled on the spiritual formation needs of the pre-service sister.

Entering the decade of the 1960s, the SFC was a vanguard movement in ecumenical, ecclesiastical, and educational trends. In the ecumenical spirit, the conference established contact with Anglican sisters in the United States and assisted them through visits to their convents, correspondence, invitations to SFC meetings and the sharing of publications. The 1962 NCEA convention theme was ecumenism and the 1963-64 Marquette workshop opened up to speakers and topics with an ecumenical outlook. The conference influenced ecclesiastics as the hierarchy of the Church from all over the world sought information on the work of the SFC. More than ever, Church leaders were asking for sister leadership in the lay movement of Catholic Action. Interest in sister formation was developing in all countries, and the leadership of the SFC was repeatedly asked to help sisters outside the United States.

> More than once we have heard from a small mission of sisters in an isolated region outside of the United States, telling us that the Sister Formation Conferences, known to them through the Bulletin, kept them in contact in spirit with their religious sisters in the United States and with the inspiring thought of the Holy See on religious life in our day.[1]

The conference's leadership and influence in educational trends continued. The SFC looked into improved nursing education, master programs in spirituality, and foundation funding for educational costs. Whether having an ecumenical, ecclesiastical, or educational dimension, ideas generated always placed the sister as the leader and the shaper of the world of tomorrow and more particularly, of the laity.

A time of tremendous transformation faced the SFC, the American woman religious, and the Catholic Church, and radical changes took place within a short span during the 1960s. Vatican Council II, starting in 1962, broke with traditional viewpoints and asked those in religious life to renew and refound. "Documents relating to major Church functions poured forth; renewal and adaptation were mandated throughout the universal Church. This provided the official green light needed by American sisterhoods to continue throughout the sixties those advances made in the fifties."[2]

Two of the council's sixteen documents, *Lumen Gentium* and *Gaudium et Spes*, were particularly important to an understanding of a new interpretation of religious life. This interpretation recognized that "the delicate balance of community and apostolate was tipped almost continually in favor of apostolate, pointing to a need for a better understanding of an apostolic spirituality, or an integration of the active and contemplative life of the religious woman."[3] The Church was now defined as the people of God with a call to build a kingdom of peace and justice. Women religious were called to work with laity and clergy in response to the needs of the poor. A third document, *Perfectae Caritatis*, gave women religious two norms for renewal; studying the Gospels and searching anew for the original spirit of their community.

Renewal already had a strong foundation in the reorganized formation programs, but, in an era marked by growing freedom and responsibility for women, the SFC was called upon to meet new challenges. American women religious, prepared to take the next step in a process that would be labelled later as revolutionizing, awakened to new responsibilities and new freedoms. "Organization structures such as habit, horarium, and community life were modified or even radically altered. To be considered as a person with social, psychological, and spiritual needs was a new experience to women schooled to taking a second place to the cause of the religious order."[4] The challenge that faced American religious women at this time was stated by Cardinal Suenens in a book, *The Nun In The Modern World*, that would be avidly read during this period:

> To restore to the religious life its original value, we must put it in harmony with the progress which has been realized in the world, and in woman's relation to that world. We must retain from the past all that is of permanent value while at the same time adapting to modern conditions. In particular, apostolic activity must be able to profit from all those positive gains which women have secured in our time. . . . To the question "What is a religious?" one ought to be able to answer, "A modern woman--not one of the eighteenth or nineteenth century--who has dedicated her life to God for the salvation of the world through the congregation to which she belongs."[5]

The struggle to define what or who an active woman religious was in the 1960s was paramount for these women. The SFC mirrored the struggles of the woman religious as it, too, sought to achieve identity, autonomy, and some power base for action. The SFC, a grass-roots organization of women religious, continued to respond to the needs of the day. With the guidance gathered from Church documents and other research and with the charismatic leadership of women, it forged ahead with projects that would have remained just ideas without the support of thousands of women religious. Although support was not always present internally among all the sisters nor externally from the many publics of religious communities, the initial vision of the SFC, that of forming the sister as an integrated woman, as a prepared professional and as an embodiment of the Church, continued to energize the group.

The SFC had moved far from the first meeting of the Committee on the Survey in 1952 when, with a six-page agenda, Sister Mary Emil stirred the small organization into action and won approval. The SFC Secretariat, now led by Sister Mary Emil's choice, Sister Annette, continued the many activities of the SFC and began new ones. Working closely with Sister Mary Emil during her first year in office, Sister Annette's leadership skills quickly established her credibility with the SFC and those associated with it. Only later and particularly over the controversy between the SFC and CMSW would Sister Annette and Sister Mary Emil come to disagree on the direction in which the SFC should be led.

Sister Annette brought much experience to her new position. She was no stranger to the activities of the SFC. She had organized a mental health institute for major superiors that was cosponsored by SFC and St. Catherine's College where she had been a professor of psychology. She had also received a grant from the Ford Foundation that allowed her to film lectures on basic psychology. These films were shared with religious communities through the SFC. Sister Annette's training in psychology made her intent on concentrating on the social and psychological aspects of the sister formation movement, and this became noticeable in the expansion of SFC issues through the years of her two terms.

The SFC came into its own as an organization to be noticed during these years. The director of the "Institute of Spirituality for Religious" to be held for the next several years at the University of Notre Dame came for advice and resources. The non-sectarian Religious Education Association asked for recommendations in choosing scholars to present Catholic views on religious education problems. The executive secretary served on committees of the Council on Cooperation in Teacher Education, the National Teacher Education Professional Standards Commission and the American Council on Education. The regional conference still drew communities together in their own areas in order to share and learn from one another. The NCEA convention was the gathering site where mothers general, directresses, and presidents of colleges discussed issues of special importance. Publications included reports of meetings and workshops, special reprints, tape recordings, and the *Sister Formation Bulletin*.

Underlying the activities between 1960 and 1964 was the growing tension between the two officially recognized organizations for sisters: the Sister Formation Conference and the Conference of Major Superiors of Women. Neither organization was meant to curtail the activities of the other, yet working in harmony was proving difficult. The very structure of each organization with its own by-laws left little room for shared areas of authority.

An important issue at this time and one that concerned both the SFC and the CMSW was the sister college. With pressure mounting from the NCEA, accrediting agencies, and communities, the SFC sought to work toward the establishment of acceptable norms for quality sister colleges. Since the philosophy of sister formation called for an excellence in education not guided by state regulations but by an effort to train members to the highest possible degree for the benefit of the person and the Church, the question was whether or not there were too many below-standard sister colleges.

Sister Colleges

Small sisters' colleges were struggling: small student bodies, meeting accreditation demands, and the financial burdens of an institution of higher learning made it almost impossible for every religious community to have its own college. The SFC found itself trying to mediate questions concerning quality in the curriculum and in the educational environment in the sister colleges that did exist. Both areas required more research, dialogue and serious decision making on the part of the SFC and each religious community. Four years after its creation, the Everett Curriculum was attacked as being too stiff and not meeting all the needs of an integrated education for sisters; namely, in the areas of the sociology, psychology, and theology. To keep up with the new developments was proving to be a mighty task, and an examination of the Marquette Workshops documents shows that SFC leadership was always looking for a better way to educate.

The discussion of educational environment initiated a great deal of serious decision-making and planning for each community at this time. Though many communities had a juniorate plan by this time, many did not. It was this concern that continued to occupy the SFC and the NCEA. Consulting services and workshops were offered by the SFC, and yet there was a great unsolved problem: how to monitor the quality of sister colleges.

Formulated at the NCEA conventions of 1959 through 1961, the personnel policies for sister college teachers were constantly examined since the quality of sister education hinged on the faculty. By 1962, the University and College Department advised that a committee study the situation and quality of sister colleges. The SFC, concerned that any outside action would indicate that the sisters themselves did not have the leadership or the training to handle this problem, asked that an SFC representative be assigned to this committee which was to set out on a plan of action.

At the August 1962 SFC leadership meeting, several moves were made to help small religious communities with their educational plans. Father William Dunne, associate secretary of the College and University Department, was requested to write a formal letter to the major superiors of women in the United States to share his concern for quality education. Through his letter, the SFC hoped to stress the educational hazard of neglecting accreditation. The SFC looked to the qualifications of accreditation as establishing a necessary guideline for sister colleges. Accrediting agencies took a specific interest in helping the sister college:

It is exceedingly difficult for such very small institutions to maintain programs and facilities adequate for regional accreditation.

Recognizing the necessity for each order to make provision for training its own members in its own principles and traditions in its own way, it would still seem possible for some form of regional inter-institutional cooperation among Catholic colleges in the same geographical area to be effected, which might well help to avoid the dissipation of limited resources and to strengthen the academic preparation of the members of the several religious communities, as well as easing problems of accreditation.[6]

Seeking the advice of the executive secretary of the National Commission on Accreditation, the SFC was told that affiliation with another institution, such as was happening with many sister colleges and Catholic University, was valuable for advice and assistance but that accreditation alone could bring the professional approval necessary for adequate recognition of the institution. "As with other institutions, these [sister] colleges require funds, they require facilities; they require teaching personnel; and they require individuals able and prepared to give strong educational leadership."[7] To help sister colleges receive accreditation, regional workshops were set up and the SFC sought to consult with any community that asked for that help.

In addition to recommending that the sister college seek accreditation, the SFC also tried to specify that the sister college should be freed from the community's internal structure and become an independent institution. To break from the tradition of this internal structure was a big step for many communities. For the sister college to be a vital part of the juniorate formation program, it was stressed that academic professionalism needed to be maintained, something difficult to do when the major superior was also the college president. Separate incorporation of the college from the religious community was recommended and would allow for separate budgeting and planning. The president and faculty of the college needed to be academically prepared for their roles and this meant the education of sisters for these positions to the level of Ph.D. Students were to be given enough time to study without the burden of community activities. These recommendations were sensible and were already followed in many communities, particularly those that had colleges serving lay women. In others, the struggle over a division of authority was exacerbated by difficulty in distinguishing between academic and community concerns.

As the higher education of women became more widespread, many religious communities opened colleges for women. This also enabled them to provide for the higher education of its own members. As these colleges sought accreditation from the secular accrediting agencies, problems soon arose because of a conflict in authority between the chief administrator and the major superior of the community. By canonical right, the major superior's authority was above that of the administrator. This became a serious obstacle which has taken many years to resolve.[8]

Some communities found it hard to understand why in-house education, something that had always worked, could not continue. Underlying this difficulty was still the struggle to understand just what integrated education meant. The given ideal condition for integrated education was the working together of college and formation personnel so that each sister would be considered an individual with particular needs and gifts. A consideration of physical and social needs was to be just as important as the right amounts of study and prayer time. Feeling strongly about these recommendations, the SFC promoted them at the seminar for administrators, held at Catholic University, and by means of personal consultation with communities.[9]

Another idea that emerged was the creation of a sister-college federation. Some believed that such a federation would bring attention to the sister college and help gather more support for the endeavor. The opposition, however, felt that this organization would hinder the sister college from meeting with other colleges and separate it in particular from its supportive connection with the Catholic woman's college. Increasing criticism spoke of the SFC as advocating a separation of sister education from the mainstream of Catholic college education. The federation was never formed, and the criticism against separate education continued.

A final practical action at this time was the creation of an educational resources committee as an arm of the SFC. This committee, whose sole purpose was to help communities with their juniorate college programs, sought "to promote cooperation and sharing of resources among Communities, and to select academic facilities and plans in harmony with the objectives of the Sister Formation Conference."[10] There were communities with sisters with Ph.D.'s who needed teaching experience, and this committee was able to serve as a clearinghouse for their placement and to help colleges fill a particular faculty need. It was suggested that the services of this committee under the leadership of Sister Augustine, OSF, and Sister Rose Dominic, SCL, be organized on a regional or state-wide basis so that a college could advise small neighboring communities on matters of accreditation and educational standards. This committee went on to investigate and to share on matters of curriculum, faculty, facilities, costs, and future planning. The Newsletter for Major Superiors was the basic organ of communication for these services.

As an effort to help administrators of sister colleges, a conference sponsored by Catholic University and directed by Sister Annette was held in 1963 and in

1964. "It is not enough to tell these communities that they may not start a college because they know that they have the right to do so. Furthermore, we must give them some assistance in working out alternative plans to that of setting up their own inferior colleges."[11]　　The conferences offered yet another opportunity for sisters to gather and discuss aspects of sister education. Presentations at the conferences dealt with faculty preparation, the relationship between college administrators and directresses of formation, and accreditation and finances of the college.

Hoping to use every avenue as a means of education for communities, the yearly NCEA conference was still seen as the time when a cross section of every community would be present. The SFC themes of the NCEA conventions of these years worked toward two goals: establishing a comprehensive view of formation and widening of the sister's vision of ministry in the Church.

NCEA Conventions

As a section of the NCEA, the SFC continued to draw selected participants to the yearly conference by the ticket-only procedure. In a letter, Sister Mary Emil shares the reasoning for this:

> In the matter of organizing the Conference, I should have said in my letter, I believe, that we have been most happy about the tri-partite representation from the communities. We allow one representative from general governance who should by all means be the major superior herself, one representative from spiritual formation--either the junior mistress, the novice mistress, or the postulant mistress, but not all three,--and a representative from the intellectual formation program. We have found that by strictly and inexorably limiting the attendance at the Conferences to just three delegates from a community, there is some nice and wholesome interest engendered in who will be selected to go. As a matter of fact, we draw more delegates by limiting the attendance than by leaving it open.[12]

Following the pattern of the previous NCEA conventions, the 1961 convention was designed to help communities plan or begin to structure a sister formation program. Major superiors and the administrators of accredited women's colleges or all sister colleges which offered off-campus or institutional branch arrangements to other communities were especially encouraged to attend so that college personnel policy matters could be further discussed. The second session of the convention dealt with a personnel policy approved the previous year. The recommendation that communities establish a norm that each year twenty percent of the juniorate 'graduates' go on to full-time graduate work was again considered. With only one percent of the 97,000 teaching sisters holding a doctorate, it was felt that there was a large source of Catholic leadership still to be tapped. The discussion led as always to the "how to": how to finance the graduate study; how to handle the situation of not being able to meet the demands of pastors who wanted sisters to fill classroom positions immediately, how to integrate the idea of the sister scholar into a religious community context.

Results of a questionnaire sent to one hundred and twenty sisters already in graduate work were shared at the convention. The central concern of these sisters was the inadequacy of their undergraduate work: "lack of sequence in courses; inadequate language preparation; haphazard 'sending away to summer school' with only vague purposes in mind; shifts in majors; philosophy and theology deficiencies."[13] To the convention attendees, these comments simply reiterated something already known: that a solid undergraduate program was needed. It was also noted that on the part of the sister herself a high level of maturity, defined as the "habit of functioning as a responsible adult," was needed for graduate study.[14]

Leaving the theme of the sister college and faculty preparation to other Conference activities, the SFC responded to a new need at the 1962 NCEA convention. Pope John XXIII's announcement of the founding of the Secretariat for Christian Unity had an immediate effect on the direction of activities in the SFC. The 1962 NCEA convention chose as its theme, "Unity of All Christians." Looking beyond the horizons of their own immediate needs, the SFC centered its main sessions on the same theme and challenged sisters to look to the needs of differing cultures and socioeconomic classes. In a letter from Augustine Cardinal Bea, head of the Secretariat for Christian Unity, the sisters were encouraged to have a real concern for contemporary problems and for Christian unity. A new mission project, the Sister Formation Overseas Project, dealing with the sponsorship of sisters from foreign countries, was discussed and further promoted. It was announced at this session that $130,000 in scholarships from colleges sponsored by sisters had already been offered to sisters from foreign countries. Orientation for these sisters was considered under the umbrella topic of the formation of the sister for her apostolic mission in the Church. It was noted that several Anglican sisters were present at this conference for the first time and by invitation of the SFC.

Flowing from the previous NCEA convention, the 1963 NCEA program centered on the general theme of "Catholic Education, Progress and Prospects." Previous themes were heard again along with a strong push for the work of the SFC to continue. Since financial backing was necessary for the effectiveness of any work, several plans were raised to help augment the financial revenue of communities: to study the stipend system in each diocese, to look into the possible subsidy program already in place in the New York diocese, and to continue to promote cooperation among religious communities. The session that dealt with intercommunity cooperation again discussed the issue of the viability of the sister college. Sister Annette wrote:

> The opposition to the all-Sisters college just now is very high--not
> as a widespread reaction--but because of the organized leadership
> of a few superiors and administrators who are determined to 'sell'
> the idea of the superiority of the mixed college under all circum-
> stances. What we have tried to do is to draw attention to the
> "Centers of Training" section of the statutes of *Sedes Sapientiae.*
> . . .I notice that the leaders of the idea of educating Sisters with
> lay students tend to ignore or deny any special role or vocation for
> the Sister. If the Sister Formation Conference were dissolved right
> now, there would be little chance for the idea of the all-Sisters'
> college to spread or maintain itself.[15]

The opposition to all-sister colleges was openly voiced at this meeting by the dean of a women's Catholic college who pleaded that the sisters should be mixed with lay students for true integrative learning. Though this was not a new opinion, the leadership of the SFC held fast to the belief that separate education was still the best mode.

At the 1964 NCEA convention which focused on "Catholic Education and National Needs," the SFC looked closely at an area that would parallel its interest in social and economic needs, already being discussed at the Marquette Workshops. "Sister Formation and Human Rights" centered on some real needs, from racial integration to combating anti-Semitism, that could be met by sisters if they were willing and able to do so. At one session, Father Matthew Ahmann declared: "Now I may be pessimistic, but I don't see much possibility of our nuns being involved in this literacy training project this summer [working in the black areas of Alabama and Mississippi]. . . .But it certainly is within the scope of the work of many of our nuns to do precisely this kind of work. . . ."[16] Sisters lacked experiential involvement in the apostolic areas now suggested. Not only had the Church at large not been identified with the struggle for human rights but the energy of sisters had been chiefly directed to large institutional works, the schools, hospitals, social agencies. It was suggested that the influence of the teaching sister in the classroom was powerful as she was able to raise the level of social consciousness among her students, but it was also proposed that perhaps the sisters could be involved in other works, works that would put them in touch with needs not met by their institutions. Sisters were being faced with new challenges, challenges that would take them from organized works of the Church to the ghettos, to marches for justice, to individual apostolates not yet explored. Even after 1964, the NCEA conventions still witnessed the nationwide gathering of sisters interested in the issues of sister formation. Sessions, however, were no longer closed and sisters in any position were encouraged to attend. This change in policy was initiated by the new leadership of the National Sister Formation Conference (NSFC). The topic for the 1965 session was "Social Reform Through Education: The Sister's Mission." It was decided at this convention that a leadership group of sorts would still serve as a clearinghouse for ideas, the orientation of new members, and the general way that new ideas were to be channeled, now through the CMSW. At this same convention, the function of the consultative committee was reviewed, and the NSFC committee favored the use of personal consultative services rather than the committee that had worked and guided the activities of SFC since 1954. The consultative committee ceased to function after April 1966. This happening was interpreted by some sisters as another way of putting the SFC under the control of the Congregation for Religious and away from the influence of the American bishops.

If the work of the NCEA conventions and the special sessions for the SFC were geared to the leadership teams of the religious communities, it was at the Marquette Workshops that college faculty were still targeted for specific education. It was stated that the purpose of the Marquette Workshops was "to explore new knowledges, especially in the behavioral sciences, for their relevance to the curriculum for the formation of Sisters, and to relate these studies to the changing apostolate."[17] The primary concern still being the education of the sister, it was deemed most important that the sister faculty be prepared for their task.

Marquette Workshops

The Marquette Workshops, begun as a means to explicate the Everett Curriculum and as a practical inservice organ for the faculties of sister students, continued to evolve. Although the 1961 session reflected on the same concerns that previous sessions had, with no session held during 1962, the 1963 and 1964 workshops took on a whole new look and direction. A new fire was evident in all SFC activities during these years, and it was at the Marquette Workshops that the sociological principles behind these changes were presented, explained, and taught.

The Marquette Workshop of 1961, "Responsibility of the Faculty for Religious-Apostolic Formation," looked again at the Everett Report and how it fit the educational needs of religious in terms of their state of life and responsibility. The Everett Report was reinforced by the apostolic constitution,

Sedes Sapientiae. Already was felt a dual tension: to either hold tight to the original curriculum or to re-investigate the curricular areas. Though only five years had passed since the report had been written, certain sections needed to be revised. As one sister active in the SFC reported, "it [Everett curriculum] was an attempt to do more than humanly possible; a theoretical curriculum that had great psychological and spiritual impact. While still in the old habit of thinking about learning, we were trying to integrate all areas of learning."[18] The criticisms pointed to the fact that there was a great stress on the intellectual in the Everett norms and that the other aspects of learning did not receive the same emphasis. The following are comments gleaned from a questionnaire administered to students attending a sister formation college during this time. Though the answers reflected experiences at only one campus, the results helped to concretize the struggle that resulted in trying to integrate the learning process. To the question, "What would you consider the strengths of the Sister Formation pro-gram?" the sisters answered: strong liberal education, integrated cultural experiences, and an academic life that was highly stressed. To the question, "What would you consider the weaknesses of the Sister Formation program?" these same sisters answered: too much pressure to succeed, physical and emotional development neglected, and isolation from the world.[19]

Reflected here were the very things that were being struggled with at the Marquette Workshops, the regional conferences and within each community. It was one thing to talk about integrative learning and it was quite another to have it happen, particularly, it would seem, in the isolation of a sister-only campus. With this in mind, it is easier to understand why the Marquette Workshops seemed to shy away from attempting to rewrite the Everett curriculum and rather took the time to look to new fields of study and to advocate the team approach in the juniorate experience and preparedness for the college faculty.

The importance and quality of the faculty and the environment in which the education of the religious was to take place were stressed in the 1961 Marquette Workshop. Special interest sessions offered were: foundations of education; general education in physical and life science; social science sequence; the Everett sequence in philosophy; instrumental use of French in the sister formation program; and the Everett sequence in psychology. Father Gambari was urged to speak at the 1961 session about the vision that women religious in the United States needed in order to do what the Church needed.

Suggestions for the 1962 workshop included having the session at successfully operating sister college centers or simply using the year's time as a re-fueling period for the sister organizers of the Marquette Workshops. The transfer of Sister Elizabeth Ann, IHM, coordinator of the workshops, to Lima, Peru, to work on the education and formation of sisters in that country brought plans for this workshop to a standstill and the 1962 session was cancelled.

A three-day "Think Session," however, did take place in the fall of 1962 for thirty selected sisters in SFC leadership. This session, led by Msgr. Ivan Illich of the Center for Intercultural Formation, Cuernevaca, Mexico, influenced the direction of the next Marquette Workshops. The days revolved around lectures, prayer, and discussion on the topic of ministry to the poor. Three sisters who had spent several months working cooperatively with sixty-seven communities in Peru came to share their experiences with the sisters. They emphasized that sisters--especially a founding group--going to another culture needed extra training to become acquainted with the new culture. The SFC was definitely coming face to face with other cultures and their needs.

Despite opposition from several SFC leaders who felt that not enough time had gone into serious study before taking a change of direction, Sister Annette forged ahead with a new vision, that of looking to the needs of other cultures. "We will certainly wish to have a workshop at Marquette during the summer session of 1963. . . .The request of the Holy See to send ten percent of our Sister personnel to Latin America is affecting all of our projects."[20] The workshop "New Perspectives in Sister Formation Curricula" bespoke well the energy and excitement of this session. The main speakers were Father Francois Houtart, director of the Center for Socio-Religious Research in Brussels, Msgr. Ivan D. Illich, Dr. Marc Tanenbaum of the American Jewish Committee, Dr. John Reidl, and Father Gambari. The reason for engaging new speakers for the Marquette Workshops was to secure experts in the developing fields of knowledge, particularly the social and behavioral sciences. The fact that the theologians were not from America indicated that these new trends were coming from outside the United States. One hundred seventy-five participants came from forty-three dioceses and represented 87,000 religious women.

In developing the theme of the workshop, attention was given to the implications for sisters coming from the deliberations and outcomes of Vatican Council II along with a consideration of the papal documents, *Mater et Magistra* and *Pacem in Terris*. These new perspectives in theology would point out another direction in the formation of sisters. Sisters would be asked to look beyond their present apostolates to new forms. "We were in the middle of the Council, no-body knew what was happening, and the thrust was whether the Sisters were only to serve the institution. For the first time that question was foremost."[21]

From the perspectives of the social and behavioral sciences, the main speakers outlined new trends and directions. Sisters were challenged to consider how their communities needed to change to meet new situations in the American culture and in foreign countries. It was projected that the individual sister would need to specialize in a particular profession and that religious communities would be called to work together on joint projects thus expanding the concept of community ministry. The word "integration" was heard again but this time with the idea of "integrating the religious and social aspects of modern life."[22] Time was spent discussing the aspects of work in Latin America. It was indicated early on that sisters were not always aware of the implications of their work and their involvement or non-involvement in the economic, social, and political arena of a country and for this reason, the study of sociology, politics, and economics was seen as more important than ever. Aspects of social change were considered with specific emphasis on the role of sisters in the cause of human rights.

Responses to the workshop were varied. Some sisters were disappointed that the old form of working directly with the Everett curriculum was not followed or that a concerted effort had not been made to update it according to the same method by which it had been written, that is, by a select group that took time to study and revise it. The approach of bringing in outside sociologists and others was viewed with some suspicion and an attitude that something precious was being lost in this cavalier attempt to present so much new material so quickly. But others spoke to the newness of the information given and the challenges raised. They were happy that they were alerted to the need of giving the junior sister a religious, sociological approach to her mission in the Church. It was mentioned that horizons were widened and a sense of urgency given in the matter of adaptation and the need to cooperate with other communities. Mainly, there was an awakening to the reality of the great social needs in the world and the great changes through which the Church and the religious in the Church must go in order to meet these needs and changes. It was as if the quality of isolation was leaving the Church and communities all at once. No longer could either say that it was not their responsibility to help.

A new study, "Institute for Juniorate Studies" also resulted from discussions at this Marquette Workshop. Through a systematic, continuing program of self-study, communities with juniorates were guided through an outline of activities, the results of which would be shared at the 1965 regional meetings. The desired outcome was that the respective roles of the juniorate directress and faculty members would become clearer along with an overall evaluation of the juniorate formation program. The outline provided reading lists and a way for communities to come together to share. This project was never implemented on a large scale due to changes in the SFC in the next few years.[23]

The 1964 session of the Marquette workshop dealt once again with the developing theology of the Church in view of the needed formation of sisters and the way new perspectives in social and behavioral sciences influenced the sister's response to needs in the Church. It was necessary to seriously study and examine the new insights brought to light as a result of Vatican II. Liberty of conscience, authority versus authoritarianism, new ecclesial structures in the Church, the mission of the Church to the poor, religious pluralisms, and liturgy reform were some of the areas examined. Particular subject areas were recognized as bridges in coming to understand these new areas; namely, the study of scripture, liturgy, theology, philosophy, psychology, and sociology. Some of the "new perspectives" recognized as necessary for an effective sister formation curricula were the study of: racial justice, moral issues connected to biological and medical developments, political situations, the changing status of women, the use of intelligence and inquiry, and biblical and liturgical development.

It was at the Marquette Workshops that sisters sought to understand what it would take to shape the future rather than to simply react to it. Exposed to avant-garde thinking, many American women religious communities took up the challenge to think and to act in new ways. Seeing sisters at the civil rights marches in Alabama, in the inner-city projects, and in new missionary endeavors would be proof of the new understanding.

The series of ten lectures of Father Francois Houtart was edited and published in 1964. *The Challenge to Change* was appropriately subtitled *The Church Confronts the Future* as Houtart attempted to survey the challenges given to the Church in the modern world. "The aim of this work is to help in the creation of a new spirit, a new dynamism, a new optimism among Christians in the present world."[24] A copy of this book was sent to every bishop in America with compliments of the SFC and the accompanying explanation:

> This work by Father Houtart is typical of the kind of studies, research, and programs which the Sister Formation Conference makes available. The services have been planned especially for superiors and for those Sister teachers and mistresses charged with the formation of other Sisters.

> This Workshop assumes, with Father Houtart, that Christianity can adapt to changing times "because it is not an ideology but a vision of the world based on revelation." It takes its orientation from the openness of the Church to all that is good as it strives to "build a bridge to the contemporary world." It is an effort to lead Sisters, not to a Crusade, but to a sense of mission based on the present opportunity to extend the loving presence of Christ within the world.[25]

The sending of this book was the last effort of the SFC in its old form to communicate with the American bishops.

When the restructuring of the SFC took place, the social concerns stated in *The Challenge to Change* were left to the individual sister to develop as the work of the new SFC settled primarily on the spiritual formation needs of the sisters.

The Marquette Workshops were not to continue after 1964. With good intentions, the SFC staff sought to keep these workshops going, yet no director was found to keep up the serious study of sister formation curriculum, and none was ever resumed. Though not recognized at the time, the need for the sister college and a unique sister formation curriculum was being seriously questioned.

The impact of the Marquette Workshops can be measured by the fact that religious communities across the United States attended the sessions from 1958 through 1964 and heard ideas that were new and innovative in education and in formation. Topics stretched from the incorporation of the Everett Curriculum into formation plans to a new understanding of social justice for the ministry of the sister.

Added to the great concern about the formation of college personnel toward an understanding of what sisters needed to know for their ministry was the SFC's concern for the formation of those sisters directly involved in the spiritual formation of the young sister. This specialized area was given attention at the workshops provided for the formation directress under the continued guidance of Father Gambari. Here the directress was given a syllabus of spiritual instruction along with helps in specific areas.

Instructional Programs in Spirituality

The Instructional Programs in Spirituality continued under the leadership of the SFC and the direction of Father Elio Gambari, SMM. As a selected expert or canonist at the Council, Gambari brought a wealth of experience to American sisters each summer. His activities with women religious now extended to Canada, England, Haiti, Italy, and India.

Nearly three hundred sisters participated in the 1961 program. They came from twenty-four states and from Belgium, Brazil, Ontario, Nova Scotia, and England. The continued purpose was the "fusion of the ascetical, intellectual, professional, and apostolic in formation within the framework of the special 'physiognomy' of each community."[26]   Since this was the third summer these workshops were given, it was hoped that each community that had been participating in these conferences would have established a spirituality curriculum, a *ratio institutionis spiritualis*. The head of the Congregation for Religious, Cardinal Valerio Valeri, addressed the conference and encouraged the sisters to continue their efforts in formation on the integration of the spiritual with the intellectual. He encouraged the sisters to follow the directives of the Church concerning the multiple elements and the progressive stages in formation as stated in *Sedes Sapientiae*. To understand the essential elements in the vocation of the sister was the challenge. Valeri also pointed out that the SFC activities were followed with interest and with approval by the Congregation for Religious.

In 1962, the Instructional Program in Spirituality was held at Mount Mercy College, Pittsburgh, and once again under the direction of Father Gambari. Among the participants were three Anglican sisters. Gambari explained that a well-planned syllabus of spiritual instruction included an integration of the spiritual and the psychological with the place of the sister in the Church's ministry as the central idea. Meshed closely with the spirit of the religious community should be formal courses in theology, scripture, liturgy and the history of the Church. The stress again was on the use and adaptation of a formation program that would cover a five-year period, postulancy through juniorate. With the growth of the juniorate movement, more and more juniorate directresses began to attend IPS.

In 1963, two workshops were held: one for those who had never been involved in IPS, and one for those who had previously attended. Father Gambari led them, and the double workshop allowed for the needs of both groups. "The Sister, Daughter of the Church" was the theme of this conference with the five-year program of formation as the core. Although evaluations of this series were always favorable, a desire was expressed for diversification of subject matter to meet differing needs of directresses.

With this in mind, the 1964 workshop, "The Religious and Her Relationship with the Church," held at Trinity College, Washington, D.C., featured Father Godfrey Diekmann, OSB and Father Gambari. Father Diekmann centered on the liturgical perspectives needed to unify instructional materials in the formation programs.

In 1964, another SFC volume was published by Fordham Press. *Religious-Apostolic Formation* by Elio Gambari and edited by Sister Cuthbert, SCMM, was a volume that gave a systematic plan for spiritual instructions, a kind of syllabus of spirituality for the formation of sisters. Published as part of the sister formation series from Fordham University Press, the book brought together the lectures of Father Gambari given at the IPS. These workshops continued under the leadership of Father Gambari and others who came to share with and instruct formation directresses even after the restructuring of the SFC.

Despite all the creative efforts of the SFC, including that of the Instructional Programs in Spirituality, it was the financial question connected with sister education that caused much concern. The very earliest survey study of 1952 had shown how communities struggled financially to provide for the needs of their sisters. Fund-raising was seen as a viable way to help in bearing the costs of adequate educational programs for sisters, particularly for graduate education.

Foundations

Sister Formation Graduate Study And Research Foundation, Inc (SFGSRF) was a project of the SFC to secure corporate funding for the graduate education of sisters. As early as January 1959, Sister Mary Emil wrote to the Raskob Foundation for Catholic Activities, Inc., with a proposal that would seek funding for the advancement of "religious, cultural, and professional formation of Sisters, on all levels."[27]   The SFC received $5000 from Raskob for operational expenses for the drive rather than for fellowships themselves. Sister Mary Emil was selected as director of the project, and after she stepped down from the leadership position of the SFC, this project along with that of consulting with small communities became her responsibility.

The plan called for a national campaign to secure funds to educate two thousand sister teachers who would in turn teach in college and train sisters for schools, hospitals, and social agencies. It was estimated that ten million dollars were needed to do this. Shortly after the project was announced *America* commented:

> Were public schools to do a proportionate job, the taxpayer would have to pay $70 million. (There are seven times more children in public schools than in Catholic schools). Think of what $70 million would do in improving the quality of public school teaching. But Congress isn't talking $70 million, it's discussing ten times that--$747 million.[28]

With emphasis on the desperate need for qualified sister college teachers, the project was approved by the National Consultative Committee of the SFC, the National SFC Committee, and the Executive Committee of the CMSW. It was believed that the Everett curriculum, though well done, had never been truly implemented across the country because there were not enough sister professors to teach it properly. Those fields particularly lacking in sister specialists were psychology, the social sciences, and philosophy. A sister graduate student could draw up to $1500 per year with a maximum of $5000 awarded to her toward her doctor's degree within three years of study. She had to be less than thirty-five years of age and would be expected to teach in a sister formation center. This center was defined as any college or college extension with a student body made up in whole or in part of sisters preparing for the three social service professions of teaching, nursing, or social work.

Francis C. Pray, vice president of the Council for Financial Aid to Education, Inc., New York, spoke at the 1961 NCEA convention about the need for this fellowship aid. Support was strong for this program because it sought to:

1.   Improve Catholic education by improving the teachers.
2.   Make the best use of investment funds because the recipients (sisters) were destined to stay in teaching for a lifetime with minimum further support needed.[29]

Two obstacles needed to be overcome if this fund-raising was to be successful. The first was an attitude that women's colleges (and in particular sister colleges) could not raise funds as successfully as other kinds of institutions. The second was the lack of fund-raising experience of many women religious. Sisters were thus urged to get involved in public affairs and to strive to acquire the business acumen needed for raising money. Two groups were established to help in the administration of SFGSRF: a lay advisory board and a college council. The lay advisory board was made up of prestigious business and industrial leaders, officers of learned and professional societies, social leaders, government officials and "a well-disposed prelate or two."[30] Cardinal Spellman gave a New York City office for the project and when the NCEA was incorporated in 1961, the SFC became authorized to receive monies under this legal instrument. It should be noted here that possible fund-raising activities was one of the reasons the SFC did not want to come under the full authority of the CMSW. To solicit funds having no official church connection was to the advantage of the SFC. The second group, the College Council, was made up of educators who met twice a year to set up guidelines for the activities of SFGSRF and to award the fellowships. The Sister Formation Graduate Study and Research Foundation, Inc. was legally incorporated as a non-profit legal entity in 1963 and recognized as an independent organization. This organization represented three hundred and seventy-seven communities, and representatives from the NCEA, SFC, and CMSW made up its board of directors.

Though many requests were made to corporations, foundations, and private persons, the response was not overwhelmingly successful. "They [foundations] were, however, dubious for the most part about giving money for a project such as this, involving only Roman Catholic Sisters, because of the possible disapproval of their constituents on religious grounds."[31] Hoping that a professional director would improve funding, a lay director was appointed in 1963. This move coincided with a July 1963 workshop for the training of sisters who would work as fund-raisers throughout the country.

The efforts made to raise money were significant, but the results were disheartening. There were small grants, the largest being a $10,000 grant from Cardinal Cushing for the support of the SF activities and $44,000 from the Maude and Louis Hill Foundation of St. Paul, Minnesota.

It was the Hill Family Foundation that financed a study aimed at setting up a unique training course in nursing with a view to raising higher professional standards in Catholic hospitals. The pilot project was to become a national demonstration center for a higher-level professional major in nursing and was backed by the National League for Nursing, the Catholic Hospital Association, and the Conference of Catholic Schools of Nursing. A summer conference involved national authorities in collegiate nursing education who reviewed the Everett curriculum as the foundation for the professional nursing major.[32]

It was the decision of the administration of the Sisters of Providence to put this project into practice at Providence Heights. Their prospective nurses would complete the B.A. curriculum prepared for teachers, but substitute the pre-nursing requirements for the purely professional courses in education. The student nurse would have an academic concentration in behavioral science. After graduation, she would transfer to the School of Nursing of Seattle University and would spend two years in a professional major leading to a BS degree in nursing, which would make her eligible for the nursing license. The Hill Foundation withdrew further funding in late 1964 due to the feeling that the project had gone as far as it could.

The Sister Formation Graduate Study and Research Foundation, Inc. (SFGSRF), was dissolved in 1965 after it was determined that the intended results were not materializing. The money left in the fund was distributed in small amounts to sisters according to the intention of the donors. To take the place of the efforts of the SFGSRF, the SFC requested that Catholic college administrators grant two graduate fellowships to sister students per year.

Through the *Major Superiors Newsletter*, superiors were also alerted to other scholarships and fellowships offered by such entities as the US Department of Education, the US Department of Health, Education and Welfare, the National Academy of Sciences. Sisters were encouraged to apply for monies according to their areas of study interest.

Aside from the two newsletters, the Sister Formation Bulletin and the Major Superiors Newsletter, the other most viable way to organize, plan, and communicate with the various communities was the work with the regional areas as set up by the NCEA. In each area there was a chairperson who worked with the SFC leadership in organizing the work of each region. The high point of each region was its annual conference.

Regional Conferences

The 1960-1961 regional conferences emphasized the apostolic trend and the need for special formation with reference to the American scene. Sister Annette presented a paper stressing the importance of juniorates following the Roman directives. In preparation for this set of conferences, communities with established juniorates had an opportunity to be interviewed so that reports of promising practices could be shared at the various regional conferences. As creatively as possible, the SFC was trying to help communities at whatever their stage in establishing the juniorate formation pattern. It was again pointed out that the book, *The Juniorate in Sister Formation*, contained basic guidance for this endeavor.

However, a different format was selected for this set of conferences: panels were used instead of prepared speeches. Those in attendance were asked to submit questions dealing with the administration, spiritual formation and intellectual formation in the juniorate. The period for free discussion was led by Sister Annette.

By now, it had been decided that the regional conferences would be meeting biennially. This allowed for more detailed preparation and also encouraged local areas to unite into sub-regions to promote home activities. The St. Louis and Southern Ohio areas were examples of active sub-regions. The 1962-63 regional conferences developed the theme of "Individual Programming for the In-Service Sister: Making Every Sister Aware of Her Potential." At these meetings there was an effort made to study the contemporary setting of the apostolic work expected of a sister. The issues of a changing society, developing technology, and escalating socio-economic problems were examined. Worksheets were used to help the participants structure for community planning with a realistic consideration of the individual talents and needs of their own sisters. The key question was whether communities were wasting spiritual, intellectual, and professional resources through a lack of continued formation of the in-service sister. Consideration of the in-service sister was not a new concern of the SFC, but a new attitude was emerging that would eventually come to be known as lifelong formation.

After the 1964 restructuring of the SFC, the regional conferences remained on a biennial schedule with the 1965 topic designated as "Christian Commitment and Church as Sacrament." The regional conferences were still the way to reach the grass-roots and as such remained a vital way to organize even the new activities of the SFC.

Sister Formation Conference Overseas Project

At the 1960 leadership meeting of the SFC, Sister Mary Josetta, RSM, had reported on a project initiated by the Sisters of Mercy of the Union. As a means of extending help to the Church in other countries, the Sisters of Mercy sought to educate junior sisters from the Archdiocese of Changanacherry, India. This type of venture was soon to be shared by many religious communities through the Sister Formation Conference Overseas Project, whereby sisters from a foreign country would be educated by a community for leadership in their own country.

Sister Josetta Butler was named chairperson of this committee in August, 1960. Communities from Africa, India, and Latin America were invited to participate. Sisters in the United States provided funding for transportation and education of these sisters. By 1961 there were twenty-three American communities helping twenty-eight foreign communities, (eighty-three sisters). Thirty colleges participated in this project.

In October of 1960, questionnaires had been sent to all major superiors asking if their community would be interested in this mission project, how many sisters they could take into their colleges, and what area/country they would be interested in.[33] Working with the United States Bishops Mission Secretariat, all American communities that had college juniorates were urged to accept yearly two sisters who had reached first profession and were able to do the academic work. Each community was further encouraged to concentrate on only one country and to give the educational opportunity to a junior sister and thus create an atmosphere for sharing between two communities.

A grant was later received from the State Department that allowed Sister Josetta and another sister to visit and survey Indian colleges. The hoped-for result was that they would be able to visit colleges that the native sisters attended before coming to America, to visit with their communities and their superiors and then come home to plan a seminar in Indian culture that would aid American faculties working with these sisters. Of concern to American sisters was the adjustment the Indian sister had to make in returning to her country.

The missionary work of American women religious in South America was also an interest of the SFC. Cardinal Cushing had given Sisters Annette and Ritamary $2000 in order to travel to Latin America in January 1962 to study the situation of sister education. After having visited communities in many of the Latin American countries, they assisted in the inauguration of a commission, analogous to the SFC, *Comite para la formacion de las Religiosas* in Lima, Peru, for the formation of religious women in Latin America. Immediately after their return, three sisters went to Peru to conduct research and to assist the new organization. This work soon coincided with other SFC projects, namely the Marquette Workshops.

With this outreach to mission work, the sisters were encouraged to come to understand the human needs of the people in other countries along with their spiritual needs. It was stressed that professional training was needed and that a strong social science foundation was required in order to understand the economic, psychological, and cultural aspects of the people they sought to serve. This recognition fit in with the growing concern of sisters to come to know the world and its needs as discussed at the Marquette Workshops and the NCEA conventions.

Restructuring of the Sister Formation Conference

The 1964 restructuring of the SFC that resulted in its becoming a committee of the CMSW was to bring years of struggle and authoritative uncertainty to an end. It is confusing and difficult to document why this "take-over" happened and many who were witness to the restructuring said it was the result of conflicting interests, differing visions, and a fight for power.

Misunderstanding between the two groups mounted as the SFC diversified its activities and broadened its efforts to bring about a new type of formation for the American sister. The major superiors did not always feel confident that the directions taken by the SFC were the best. This was evident in the dissatisfaction expressed over the change in focus of the Marquette Workshops and in the CMSW rejection of the SFC plan to be a department in the NCEA.

The major superiors wanted more to say about the SFC and its works, and yet the SFC wanted to stay clear of the authority of the CMSW. The autonomy sought by the SFC was viewed as necessary if the work of the conference was to continue. It had been shown time and again that the major superiors did not always know enough about the workings of the SFC to push the educational programs forward.

While the two leadership groups were trying to determine what authority each would have, a third group, the Congregation for Religious, was there to make the final decision as to who was to have the greater power. That there was conflict was evident by the barrage of letters exchanged between CMSW and SFC leadership at this time. Well aware of the confusing situation, Sister Annette took steps early in her tenure in office to follow Sister Mary Emil's careful plan to keep the SFC independent of the CMSW. Writing to Mother Mary Consolatrice, BVM, chairman of the CMSW, she asked that the relation of the SFC to the NCEA and the CMSW be clarified. She asked that more direct communication be established between the two groups and that both sets of by-laws specify the authority of each group.

It appears that SFC performs certain functions, initiates certain projects, plans certain workshops, and the like, all of which are designed to improve the spiritual, intellectual, and professional formation of Sisters. In planning these functions, projects, workshops, etc., SFC has in mind the wishes of the major superiors. The major superiors cannot perform these functions themselves and at the same time fulfill their many duties as major superiors. The major superiors, in delegating the responsibility for Sister Formation projects to SFC, do not give away any of the power and responsibility which is theirs. They merely delegate it as they always do when local superiors discharge their duties locally or the novice or junior mistresses perform their duties in their particular area.[34]

No action was taken at this time toward further communication other than what had previously been established through the liaison committee of the CMSW. Seeking to strengthen the relationship of the NCEA and the SFC, the SFC leadership sought to move the SFC from the status of a section under the college and university department to that of a separate department. The thinking behind this was that religious men had a separate department but not religious women. Sister Annette voiced it well:

> I understand from Father Dunne that the executive committee of the college and university department viewed with favor the request of the SFC that it be given departmental status in the NCEA. This would give us the same status as the department of superintendents, as the major seminary department, or the minor seminary department. It would mean that a Sister could take the lead in setting up the programs without clearing it with a layman. I think at this stage in our consciousness in our role in the Church, this is essential in order to clarify the relation between religious and lay people. I know that this request has not been brought to the executive board of the NCEA because they would have the final vote on it, and I am sure that they would turn it down without some pressure from the Conference of Major Superiors of Women.[35]

That vote of confidence never came from the CMSW. Mother Mary Consolatrice's answer was cloaked with some mystery as to who advised them not to support the issue:

> During our meetings the question arose again concerning the SFC asking for department status in the NCEA. Since we have been advised that such action would not be advantageous and wise at this time, the National Committee decided therefore that the SFC should withdraw all requests for such status. We are under the impression that nothing definite has been done recently, and hence we would appreciate letting the matter rest until further notice.[36]

Although difficulties seemed to escalate between the two groups, the activities of the SFC continued. Letters between the two groups demonstrated that the misunderstanding had to do with who had the final authority in decision-making and who in effect was to take credit for the decisions. Some objections lodged against the SFC were recorded in this letter to Father Gambari by Sister Annette:

> We are very much disturbed because the chief difficulty seems to be arising within our own ranks. Rev. Mother Kathryn Marie, vice chairman, stated that Sister Formation had always been a part of the Conference of Major Superiors--a committee or unit part of it; and that blessings could only come by SFC operating under obedience to the Conference of Major Superiors. We [SFC leadership] indicated (1) that the Conference [SFC] was and is an organization in its own right, but subject to the CMSW according to the terms of the arrangements mutually agreed upon in the presence of two members of the Sacred Congregation of Religious; and (2) that it is not here a question of "religious obedience", but of authorization under competent authority, having a veto power and a power to approve new initiatives of our distinct organizations.[37]

The CMSW held that in a June 1962 letter from Cardinal Valeri and Archbishop Philippe, the Congregation for Religious insisted that associations or works concerned with matter pertaining to religious life were morally subject to the CMSW. This statement varied little from the letter issued at the time of the organization of the CMSW.[38] Wanting to explain that the SFC was under the direction and control of the Conference of Major Superiors, the CMSW used the letter as an occasion to state that their Roman advisors felt the SFC should be directly under the CMSW.

With the feeling that the SFC was about to be suppressed, great agitation began within the Sister Formation Conference.

> It is a source of great anguish to us that we can never discuss with the officers of the CMSW the projects in which we are engaged and which have such significance for the welfare of Sisters and the Church. We have wanted to collaborate with the CMSW in some of these projects since it would enhance charity among communities and advance our good works immensely. But, before we can bring these considerations into our discussions, we are enmeshed in legalistic questions which, so far as we can determine, are of no importance in the realm of charity. They do serve, however, to consume many hours of precious time, and to take us away from work which is crucial not only for the Church

in the United States but also in other parts of the world, especially Latin America. In that sense, these constant and petty harassments strike us as being fundamentally evil.[39]

The Congregation for Religious responded to the controversy between the SFC and the CMSW by sending representatives to the 29 August 1963 joint meeting of the CMSW and SFC leadership. Archbishop Paul Philippe and Father Bernard Ransing were present. The heart of the meeting was a detailed examination of the work of the SFC along with another look at the working relationship between the CMSW and the SFC. Special attention and scrutiny was given to an article by Sister Annette that appeared in the spring issue of the *Sister Formation Bulletin* entitled "The Local Superior as Spiritual Leader," along with all that had been printed in previous issues of the *Bulletin*. Apparently there had been concern communicated to the Congregation for Religious by some major superiors that Sister Annette's article which stressed that a superior could not act as the conscience of her sisters was not in keeping with the teachings of the Church. After interviewing Sister Annette and Sister Ritamary as representatives of the SFC and examining the *Sister Formation Bulletin*, Bishop Philippe gave high praises to the work of the SFC and approval of all that had been published in the *Bulletin*. Despite this approval, he explained that the Congregation for Religious prescribed that the SFC should come under the jurisdiction of the CMSW because of the importance of formation being under the direct responsibility of the major superiors. According to the official minutes of the meeting, the bishop determined that the SFC would best be a commission of the CMSW:

> They [the major superiors] cannot let this formation [to train or form their sisters] out of their control or supervision. . . .Since the time of the organization of the Conference of Major Superiors it is evident that something should be organized in order to keep the divine rights of the office or duty given by God.[40]

Confusion abounded after this meeting both because different versions of the minutes of the meeting were circulated around the country. and because there was no agreement among some SFC and CMSW leadership about the exact decision of the Congregation for Religious. The leadership of the SFC had interpreted the visit as approval to continue in an autonomous manner. "You will be happy to know that the Sister Formation Conference has received a renewed and complete approval from the Holy See, covering its programs and purposes. . . ."[41] wrote Sister Annette. The leadership of the CMSW on the other hand quickly published contrary news, "You will be pleased to know that in a meeting of the National

Executive Committee of the Conference together with the national officers of Sister Formation and its Executive Secretaries, Archbishop Philippe raised Sister Formation to the status of a commission of the Conference of Major Religious Superiors."[42]

Because of these misunderstandings and problems of communication between the SFC and CMSW leadership, the CMSW soon issued a letter stating that plans were underway to study the present situation and how the changes were to take place.[43] The CMSW definitely took the lead and with approval from Rome. The SFC had no choice but to follow and no authority with which to object. Letters were written by some SFC leadership to Archbishop Philippe, Father Gambari, and to American bishops about the situation, but no action was taken to protect the SFC from the rewriting of its by-laws.

A later meeting of the National Sister Formation committee and CMSW national officers worked on the restructuring process to be completed by August of 1964 for the National Sister Formation Conference. Mother Mary Regina, RSM, noted:

> His Excellency's [Archbishop Phillipe] plan calls for an increase of personnel in the National Committee of S.F.C. to twelve members, six of whom will be Major Superiors to be elected by Major Superiors in open national elections from nominees who are particularly qualified to serve in the continual development in excellence of S.F.C., who are also dedicated to its interests, and who will have declared their readiness to serve S.F.C. The other six members may or may not be Major Superiors. They will be elected according to the traditional plan of elections for the National Sister Formation Committee nominees in which by due procedures candidates are presented who are particularly qualified by their special gifts, academic documentation, their experience and dedication to secure to S.F.C. by their service the richest development of its works. . . .In the light of Archbishop Philippe's plan, the National Committee of S.F.C. will remain the same as to status and function in N.C.E.A.[44]

At this meeting, a committee made up of CMSW and NSFC members was appointed with the task of rewriting the by-laws. One of the sisters on the by-laws commission wrote, "I think one of the difficulties in the background of Sister Formation has been the sort of deliberate ambiguity as to the duties and functions of certain officers."[45] After this rewriting there would be little room for ambiguity and little room for any leadership without the firm control of the major superiors. Many sensed that the new by-laws would eliminate the need for a consultative committee of priests and religious men and for a working relationship with the NCEA. Losing contact with these two groups appeared just another disastrous blow to the continued work of the SFC. If this were to happen, it was seen as "a strong stand on the conservative side of wanting to remove the organization [SFC] from any ties with the American Bishops and put it directly under the control of the Roman Curia, with no checks or balances."[46]

A letter written by Sister Mary Emil to the national chairperson of the SFC, Mother Mary Regina, gave a final permission for the contemplated action of restructuring. This original architect of the SFC wrote:

> After much thought and prayer on our meeting of last week, in St. Louis, it seems to me that I should send you this statement to be used by you in any way you see fit. The legal, and in fact, the only policy-making body of Sister Formation as it now exists as an entity having a double dependence on CMSW and NCEA, is the National Sister Formation Committee. . . .As a single member of the committee I should like, by this letter, to put on record these beliefs, which I feel are shared by a majority of our committee, but on which they would naturally have to speak for themselves.

> 1.   There is no present conflict or conflict of interest between the Sister Formation Conferences and the Conference of Major Superiors of Women.
> 2.   The plan originally put forth by His Excellency, Archbishop Philippe, for which the two groups have now prepared tentative proposed by-laws to be offered to the Sacred Congregation for Religious and to the Major Superiors assembled in their annual meeting of 1964, is well calculated not only to preserve all needed autonomy for SFC, in dependence upon CMSW, and all desirable relationships with NCEA, but to strengthen the work of Sister Formation.
> 3.   The Mothers and Sisters now attempting to stabilize and clarify relationships between the two organizations are acting in loyalty and good faith and deserve our gratitude and cooperation.[47]

With this statement of support written by a woman who had at one time felt so strongly about the needed independence of the SFC from the CMSW now being circulated freely among the NSFC committee and later among all the major superiors, the die was cast. The revolution that Sister Mary Emil had led was now being publicly ended by her letter. Perhaps she felt that necessary goals had been met and now it was time to limit change. All but one major superior would agree to the new plan at the August meeting. Msgr. Hochwalt too agreed that the SFC should be under the CMSW. By 1964, the NCEA had decided it would no longer financially support the SFC. Said Msgr. Hochwalt:

> I will stake my reputation on the assumption that the movement under the careful guidance of the Major Religious Superiors of Women will continue for a long indefinite future and will accomplish what it set out to do originally without a proliferation of understaffed institutions whose well-trained teachers should be doing a job for all of Catholic education rather than a handful of the elite.[48]

The change of status did not take place, however, without some serious protests. Many sisters felt that to become a committee of the CMSW was to suffer the fate of being dissolved. Viewed by some sisters as a political move that gave the major superiors more power and the grass-roots less, the Congregation for Religious was looked upon as the dealer of the death blow.

> It is, however, safe to hazard the guess that the Sister Formation Conference has been caught up into the same kind of political struggle as that taking place at the Council, in which the Pope and the majority of Bishops are trying to de-centralize, and the Curia is trying to centralize even more. All of the people involved, I am sure, are doing what they think is for the good of the Church. But, in the process, the Sister Formation Conference, as a semi-autonomous group, comprising all of the religious communities of women of the country, and having sectional status in the College and University Department of the NCEA, has disappeared. Instead, we have the promise of a committee on Sister Formation in the CMSW, but how it will be secured is not clear.[49]

On August 26, 1964, the revised by-laws were enacted. The new National Sister Formation Committee comprised of six major superiors elected by and from the CMSW and six sisters selected at large from the SFC was led by a newly named executive secretary. Along with a new editor of the *Sister Formation Bulletin*, the NSFC also changed locations. In the fall of 1964, the SFC office moved from the NCEA headquarters to the CMSW headquarters. The reason given was that now all services to sisters could be consolidated. For many this physical move signified the change of emphasis of the NSFC. The move, cemented by a change in the by-laws of the SFC, placed this grass-roots movement into a structure that no longer allowed for the same kind of creative and almost serendipitous action that had been characteristic of the SFC.

Certainly, the Congregation for Religious and the major superiors had gotten their way. Archbishop Philippe said during the 1963 meeting that, "This SFC has a function which is very good in itself but it looks to the Mothers General and Provincials in this country. The relationship should be more functional and perfect."[50] Making the SFC become more functional and perfect was a tall order for the CMSW to fill. The SFC had tried to be both functional and perfect by its unique form of joining formation, education, and leadership personnel in its decision-making and program development. This leadership style foreshadowed new forms of government and shared decision-making in religious life. The transfer of the SFC to the CMSW took the initiative of planning out of the hands of the sisters and put it back into the hands of leadership. What Archbishop Philippe termed a step forward,"This [SFC under CMSW] will strengthen, give more solid ground, give the satisfaction of being in the hands of the Superiors instead of running alone,"[51] would be judged by others as a return to the past.

Conclusion

"You could see the chapter was going to close anyway. It would have been nicer if it had closed a little more quietly."[52] So spoke one of the early SFC pioneers about the last years of the SFC before coming under the CMSW. There was no doubt the SFC as it had first been envisioned had been dissolved. The CMSW as the official body representing American women religious had succeeded in bringing the structure of the SFC under its complete jurisdiction. Sister Annette wrote something approaching a eulogy:

> Those of us who knew the situation take comfort in the belief that the idea of Sister Formation is out and can never be retracted. Perhaps the Sister Formation Conference as we have known it has done its work. All of us who have been caught up in this great movement are deeply grateful to God for permitting us, if only for a short time, to serve the entire Church and our country through the Sister Formation Conference.[53]

At the time it may have seemed that the institutional had won out over the charismatic, yet the SFC in its first ten years of existence had gained tremendous victories for the individual woman religious. The struggle to recognize the needs and talents of the woman religious and allow for the proper education of that woman brought into being new forms of integrative learning to religious formation and new ways to serve in the ministry.

To study the SFC, its birth and growth, is to study the movement of change among American women religious. By means of the SFC, limiting structures were questioned so that religious communities could better prepare for a change that was bound to come. With forward-looking planning, not only was professional preparedness stressed but graduate study was considered a necessity and all this in the context of the integration of the professional with the spiritual.

The birthing process of the SFC was difficult, and so were its many stages of growth and, finally, its time of transformation into another religious organization. It was as if change and adaptation were to be the watchwords of the work of American women religious. A sister recalling the trauma of the first questionnaire to communities for the 1952 survey shared this: "We took it in hand and did the best we could. It was like stepping out into the future and into the unknown, and we had to be willing to admit that we had something to learn."[54] Indeed much learning went on in the ten years documented between that historic survey and the closing of an unprecedented of the SFC chapter in the history of American women religious.

Sister Annette summarized the constant challenge that would remain for sisters in America even after the initial work of the SFC had passed on to communities now able to carry that work forward and to different organizations representing American women religious:

> Consequently, if we are to form Sisters for this particular time in the history of the Church, we must be concerned about the part Sisters will play in building this bridge to the contemporary world. This purpose places in consoling perspective the fundamental nature of religious life, which gives primacy but not separateness to the spiritual life; which is intrinsically orientated to God in a spirit of detachment, but which remains sensitive to the needs of the world in dedicated service. Any attempt to separate the spiritual from life in this world is contrary to the idea from which the Sister Formation Movement derives its dynamism in the Church. As you know, this basic idea of Sister Formation has permeated all of the programs of the Sister Formation Conference as well as the formation programs of individual communities that have been guided by the ideals of the Sister Formation Movement. Religious life, viewed in this perspective, calls for an integration

of the spiritual, intellectual, professional and apostolic dimensions of the Sister's formation.[55]

For all American women religious the challenge was to work out what genuine, effective ministry means in the modern world.

CHAPTER VI   CONCLUSION

What has happened today to the structures, the juniorates and colleges, the curriculums, and other activities begun by the SFC? Where are the sisters who experienced the richness of the pre-service sister formation training? It would be hard today to find many sister formation colleges, much less a curriculum earmarked for sister formation. Yet to track the power and influence of sister formation in American communities and among the women of this era is to understand that "there are no ideas and no institutions that can be insulated from history. Not only must the Church and the Christian adapt to 'the signs of the times,' it must recognize its own profound involvement in the historical process."[1] The SFC was outstanding in the historical process of change that American women religious experienced in the 1950-1960s.

The Church in the 1950s

The Catholic Church in America in the 1950s had arrived at the end of an immigrant journey. By 1960, Catholics were no longer looked upon as aliens and outsiders but had been assimilated into the mainstream of American life. Focused on the needs of its own, a world within a world, the Church had for too long experienced isolation as the way of survival. Its organizations--professional, social, educational, and intellectual--and its doctrine had told the rest of America that it was unique and insulated and able to survive as an American subculture without becoming a part of the whole. Despite this experience, the Church was able to provide for its people a vehicle for Americanization through the unique Catholic educational system. Within this educational system, Catholics learned what it would take to be successful in American culture. It was the demand for "a creative leadership attuned at once to the needs of a Catholic people passing through a period of profound social change and to the demands of a revitalized Christianity," that brought a new openness and freedom to the Catholic Church.[2]

129

This new openness and freedom deeply affected the lifestyle of American women religious.

Catholics were brought quickly into the American mainstream by "the large scale entry of Catholics into the middle class during and after World War II, the opportunity for higher education opened to Catholic veterans by the GI Bill of Rights, the election of a Catholic president and the work of an ecumenical council."[3] Into a highly structured and dynamic American society, they spread from the city to the suburbs, from blue collar to white collar jobs, from high school to graduate studies thus causing an opening to and exposure of Catholics to the world. The Church and its ministers were at the same time called to widen their visions and works beyond the local parish and the school to that of a world outside the confines of the Catholic Church.

Within a short period of time, the American Catholic Church was faced with the challenge of meeting the needs of the twenty-first century. A new relationship between the Church and the broader culture was capsulized in the title of a document issued from Vatican Council II, "The Church in the Modern World." The Church was openly saying that it belonged in the modern world and wanted to relate and give service to this modern world. Catholics went quickly "from the frozen immobility of the counterreformation and entered the relatively open dialogue of the ecumenical age."[4] Vatican Council II heightened the acceleration for change and reform in the Church. However, the taking of risks, experimenting, and ferment for change had been long in coming and was evidenced in the work, research and searching that American women religious experienced even before the Council.

As the Church recognized the need to change, so too did its ministers. American women religious, the single largest group of Church ministers in America took renewal and adaptation very seriously. The challenge to come into the twenty-first century called for and resulted in a new model of religious living. Encouraged to become "Nuns in the World," they examined their lifestyle, government structures, formation models, and customs to make their way of life relevant and less isolated in order to meet the needs of the day and in keeping with the original spirit of each group.

The Passing of an Age

"The time of isolation is past. There are no longer private islands in the world or in the Church, either geographically or culturally."[5] The years of the SFC parceled a time of turmoil and crisis in the world, the Church, and in religious life. It was at this time that American women religious began to emerge from a monastic tradition in a closed Church system to an open system with new apostolic emphasis that included international outreach in the 1960s. The momentum that enabled the American woman religious to become that integrated woman, prepared professional, and embodiment of the Church was exemplified in the work of the Sister Formation Conference. This conference was a vehicle for institutional change, an organization that prepared women religious for the changes advocated by Vatican Council II. The 1960s witnessed the disintegration of many of the structures of the SFC and a time when many women religious left their communities for various reasons, yet the significance of the SFC was its ability to be a model for growth.

> And yet the influence of Sister Formation on the church in the United States is massive and continuing, in the women who remain in religious life as well as many lay leaders in our educational and health systems, in pastoral ministry and work in the public sphere. Through the Bulletin, and its educational initiatives, especially through the new vision imparted to apostolic goals, Sister Formation challenged mediocrity in religious life and service, and, at the same time, introduced a humanizing self-respect, respect for the God-given talents of others, and a concern for loving relationships. Most of all, Sister Formation lives in the fact that it developed a biblically and theologically literate population, ready for the new teachings of the Second Vatican Council.[6]

The integrated formation that was the ideal of the SFC enabled sisters to distinguish and understand the problems of a world society and energized them to minister in this society using the existing tools of the day.

By examining the trends in religious life during the first ten years of the SFC in a context of sociological principles, some understanding of the patterns and processes of religious life can be had. "Dependence, conformity, and institutionalized functionalism were hallmarks of pre-Vatican II religious life. . . . Responsibility, community-building, and discernment of gifts are the emerging ideals."[7]

American women religious acted in an independent manner when dependence was expected, particularly in a Church where women were not viewed as aggressive. They formed their own organization and worked against great obstacles to raise the professional standards of sisters within the Church and in the public eye. Providing their own grass-roots leadership, they began to exert pressure for changes. Not only did they encourage proper education and credentialing but also creativity and recognition of the individual.

The SFC represented a work group having key ideas and joined together to accomplish a task in an organized and systematic manner. Wilfred Bion in his research concerning group and organizational behavior spoke of the difference of a work group from an assumption group, each of these groups typifying the factions within and without religious life at this time. The SFC work group brought everyone together in order to solve the problems of the day, thus believing in the wisdom of the group. The assumption group could be characterized as those sisters and others who believed there was no need for change. This group believed that the individual was fully equipped by instinct and position to play a part in the group's activity and that no other work or individual initiative was needed. Further, this latter group would see no reason for group action since the leader knew everything and was in charge. Tension and misunderstanding occurred as these two groups confronted one another with differing solutions to the problem of sister education.

The working together demanded by the SFC caused religious communities in America to unite as never before to work together toward a common goal. The SFC sought to work within a demanding situation rather than flee from the thought of change and adaptation.[8] There was an urgency in the task placed before women religious to update, and this concentration on a task engendered a spirit of working together that brought down artificial barriers between communities of women. Dealing with external and internal factors, the goal of educational equality was sought for all sisters. Leadership quickly arose from the ranks, the SFC was established, and a network for group work and sharing was established. The external pressures of increasing state certification demands and a rapidly changing world that needed to be ministered to in new ways caused sisters to look beyond their own communities as a norm. Internal pressures came from a keen desire to follow the directives of Church leaders and documents and from the growing recognition of the needs of the individual person.[9]

American religious women expressed a willingness to change their customs and ways of living to meet a new call to service. Remaining strong readers of the signs of the times, these women responded to the needs of the day and recognized that education was the main tool needed to facilitate the transition to new ways of ministry. Believing that education liberated and building on existing tradition, these women religious reexamined and experimented with the education and formation systems that prepared them for ministry. In a systematic way, with the help of research, study, and experimentation, a new form of integrated education was introduced.

Depending no longer on the belief that a person with a call was fully prepared by only God's grace, the needs of the individual were recognized, and each sister was encouraged to develop her skills, personal and interpersonal. This was indeed a breakthrough in thinking for many. Now every sister was to be given the opportunity to receive full professional training.

Tradition and custom were changed in this movement as charismatic and grass-roots leadership occupied positions once held only by those given the office of authority. It was those sisters who already experienced graduate education and the pull to integrate the intellectual with the spiritual who became the charismatic leaders of the SFC. It was the challenge of offering this same experience to their own sisters that became the goal of the SFC.

Education and the new forms of formation would open religious life, long kept a closed system by tradition and by canon law, to new ways of living and put the sister into contact with reality as never before. Enclosure had been the chief characteristic of the contemplative life imposed on active communities. Communities had found it hard to live separated from the world and yet do apostolic work which demanded certain contacts with the world. With this emphasis on withdrawal from the world, the sister had been allowed to serve, but in a limited capacity. Canon lawyers had managed to codify religious life on the basis of the cloistered sister so that the daily schedule, habit, and expectations of an apostolic sister were limited. Struggling to achieve a proper balance between prayer and ministry was part of the task facing religious at this time.

The SFC did indeed help to change the patterns and processes of education and formation in the communities of American women religious and brought sisters into the twenty-first century. By 1966, 90,091 sisters in America out of 173,866 had at least one degree; fifty-eight percent with a bachelor's, twenty one percent with a master's degree, and two percent with a doctorate. In 1984, 98,143 had a college degree, forty-three percent with a master's and two percent with a doctorate.

The change in patterns and processes affected not only the educational standards of the sister but also affected her life as a person. Intent on more than just internal reorganization, sisters strove to excel in service to others. The recognition of the sister as a professional, a person, and as a woman of the Church during these years could be hailed as a progressive step for all women. American women religious, a unique group of women, were a part of the early stirrings of the women's movement in the United States. Finding themselves bound by rules and a vision of what "good sisters" were: docile, obedient, and submissive, they had to forge a new image wherein they could exercise decision-making, leadership, and effectiveness in a male-oriented Church. This transformation did not come easily. Answering the growing need of the individual person to exercise her talents and gifts and listening to a Church asking for a more professional and enlightened leadership were the guiding principles for these women.

Final Thoughts

The Sister Formation movement began with the one goal of allowing Sister Lucy to become spiritually enriched, "psychologically mature, intellectually disciplined, broadly cultured and professionally competent."[10] Following the directive from the Church to renew and renovate, these women began a process of regeneration that is still happening. The Sister Formation Conference challenged American women religious to new growth, a new vision, and introduced new ways of coming to understand the Sister as person. Though there were misunderstandings and conflicts and even personal quarrels in the SFC, a purpose was served. Sisters learned that they had to fight for the right to be professionally and personally prepared for their life of service. They experienced that the development of their intellectual life was as important as that of their spiritual life and that to be professionally prepared was an act of justice to students and all they served.

The irony behind the successful work of the Sister Formation Conference was that through this vehicle of change, American women religious reached a new professional level only to find that the Church was not ready to accept a mature and psychologically strong group of women. Changes occurred and frustration was generated because Church and community structures did not change with the same rapidity as American women religious changed. No longer able to function within a lifestyle that called for docility and little initiative, sisters came to understand that leadership, competence, and a sense of risk were needed to meet ministry and personal needs. "The specialization of all areas of ministry--education, health care, and social service work--made it increasingly difficult to treat women religious as a collection of interchangeable parts."[11] In reforming and renewing themselves, American women religious outgrew their pre-determined structural niche in the Church, that of "silent but efficient pillars of the Catholic school system and hospital network."[12]

These women were no longer an anonymous group but mature women seeking to live within community and to experience personal rights that exceeded the former group identity of "Sister." The very Church authorities that had encouraged education and a working together of communities and religious superiors who had sought to implement needed changes were unprepared to deal with a liberated group of women desiring to exercise leadership in society, the Church and their own lives. Caught in a time when the institutional models of Church and religious life were quickly disintegrating and other more practical models were not yet in place, the structure of religious life was looking for "a new paradigm characterized by greater concern for the individual and an attempt to achieve a greater balance of individual and community values. Sisters' values are no longer totally consistent with the hierarchical model: nuns seek autonomy and self-definition, freedom, commitment to key issues, affirmation of themselves as change agents."[13]

The interpretation of authority, of who was to have it, and how it was to be exercised, were the elements of paradox in these structural transformations. As American women religious searched for an active role in the Church, the institutional model of Church restricted leadership to a select male clerical group. With the promulgation of the new code of canon law on 25 January 1983, (thirty years after the founding of the SFC), religious life became less legally defined by the Church. The many particulars of religious life previously delineated by two thousand separate laws were reduced to one hundred seventy-three laws. This change of attitude demonstrated a change of thinking in the Church. With a change of emphasis from external regulations, the new code emphasized religious life as a following of Christ in order to serve one's fellow human being. As women religious sought to refashion the structures of religious life, they often found the call of tradition pulling them back to former ways. While external structures in community and in the Church were challenged to change, sisters--individually and in communities--refashioned their relationships to society, to Church, and to laity. Leaving behind the cloistered life-style, they began to exercise a freedom of action and thought in new views of ministry that concentrated on issues of justice, new works of mercy, and the recognition of the need to work in partnership with the laity. The essentials remained in religious life while these women adapted to a changing social scene.[14]

The challenge of renewal and adaptation, a constant call in the history of the Church, placed these women as prophets and models to the whole Church. Heralding the need for change, they sought to modernize their way of living while calling for the whole Church to do likewise. They empowered one another by a recognition and respect of personal gifts and allowed shared responsibility and decision-making to become their mode of governance. With a new consciousness of themselves as persons and women, they built a new structure within their religious groups based on the concept of community. This new concept included living, praying, and working together, and helping others to do the same. The laity, the Church, and the poor needed models of community built on an appreciation of the person rather than on a basis of hierarchical principles.

"Operation Bootstrap" and "Operation Airlift" were terms used early in the history of the Sister Formation Conference by Sister Mary Emil to describe the need for sisters to work together to bring themselves into the modern world. Now American women religious, touched in various ways by the force and happenings of the last years, find themselves in a Church that is only beginning to understand their vision of community, of ministry to the poor, of their need to be recognized as equals. The Church encouraged American women religious to be professionally credentialed in order to be effective in their ministries. This was praiseworthy, but the greater task now is to fashion a structure within the Church that will recognize the total gift of these women.

The works and life-style of American women religious in recent years stand as a bold testimony to the energy and vision of the early pioneers of the Sister Formation Conference. "Sister Lucy" has earned the opportunity to be an integrated woman, a prepared professional, and an embodiment of the Church.

ABBREVIATIONS

Women's Religious Communities

ASC	Adorers of the Blood of Christ
BVM	Sisters of Charity of the Blessed Virgin Mary
CHM	Congregation of the Humility of Mary
CR	Sisters of the Resurrection
CSC	Sisters of the Holy Cross
CSJ	Sisters of St. Joseph
DC	Daughters of Charity
FCSP	Sisters of Charity of Providence
IHM	Servants of the Immaculate Heart of Mary
OP	Sisters of St. Dominic
OSB	Benedictine Sisters
OSF	Franciscan Sisters
RSM	Sisters of Mercy
SC	Sisters of Charity
SCC	Sisters of Christian Charity
SCL	Sisters of Charity of Leavenworth, Kansas
SCMM	Sisters of Charity of Our Lady, Mother of Mercy
SFCC	Sisters for Christian Community
SL	Sisters of Loretta
SND	Sisters of Notre Dame de Namur
SNJM	Sisters of the Holy Names of Jesus and Mary
SP	Sisters of Providence
SSND	School Sisters of Notre Dame
SSS	Sisters of Social Service

Men's Religious Communities

CM	Congregation of the Mission
CSC	Congregation of Holy Cross
CSSp	Congregation of the Holy Ghost and Immaculate Heart of Mary
CSSR	Redemptorist Fathers
CSV	Clerics of St. Viator
FSC	Brothers of the Christian Schools
OFM	Franciscan Fathers
OP	Orders of Preachers
SJ	Society of Jesus (Jesuits)
SMM	Montfort Missionaries

NATIONAL CONSULTATIVE COMMITTEE
NATIONAL SISTER FORMATION COMMITTEE

	'54	'55	'56	'57	'58	'59	'60	'61	'62	'63	'64	'65	'66
NATIONAL CONSULTATIVE COM													
Fr. Bryan J. McEntegart	X	X	X	X	X-off								
Msgr Frederick Hochwalt	X	X	X	X	X	X-off	X	X	X	X	X	X	X
Msgr John J Voight	X	X	X	X	X-off	X	X	X	X	X	X	X	X
Fr. C Reinert, S.J.	X	X	X	X	X	X-off							
Fr. Allan Farrell, S.J.	X	X	X	X	X	X-off							
Fr. Cyril Meyer, C.M.	X	X	X	X	X	X	X-off						
Fr. John Murphy	X	X	X	X	X-off								
Msgr. Henry C Bezou		X	X	X	X	X	X-off						
Br. Walston Thomas, F.S.C.		X	X	X	X	X	X-off						
Fr. A A Lemieux, S.J.					X	X	X	X-off	X-sa	*			
Fr. Francis J O'Neill, C.S.S.R.					X	X	X	X-off	X-sa	*			
Br. Bonaventure Thomas, F.S.C.					X	X	X	X	X	X	X	X	X
Fr. William J. Dunne, S.J.						X	X	X	X	X	X		
Fr. Elio Gambari, S.M.M.						X	X	X	X	X	X	X	X
Msgr. James T Curtin							X	X	X	X	X	X	X
Fr. Frederick A McGuire, C.M.							X	X	X	X	X	X	X
Fr. Joseph F. Gallen, S.J.									X	X	X	X	
Fr. Celsus Wheeler, O.F.M.									X	X			
Fr. John J Wright									X-Bf	X-Bf	**		
Msgr. Elwood C Voss										X	X	X	X
*stayed on at request of S. Annette													
**BThomas took his place													
	'54	'55	'56	'57	'58	'59	'60	'61	'62	'63	'64	'65	'66
NATIONAL SR FORMATION COM													
Sister Mary Emil, I.H.M.#	X	X	X	X	X	X	X	X	X	X			
Sister Mary Basil, S.S.N.D.	X	X	X	X	X								
Sister Celine, C.R.	X	X	X	X	X								
Sister M. Emmanuel, O.S.F.##	X	X	X	X	X	X	X						
Mother Mary Florence, S.L.	X	X	X	X	X	X	X						
Sister M. Gerard, O.S.F.	X	X	X	X	X								
Sister Mary Richardine, B.V.M.	X	X	X	X	X	X	X	X	X				
Sister Ritamary, C.H.M.								X	X	X	X		
Mother Annamaria Dengel, S.C.M.M.		X	X	X	X	X							
Sister Frederica Horvath, S.S.S.		X	X	X	X								
Sister Judith Lang, F.C.S.P.			X	X	X	X	X	X	X				
Sister Augustine, O.S.F.				X	X	X	X	X	X				
Sister Bertrande, D.C.				X	X	X	X						
Sister Jerome, O.S.B.				X	X	X							
Mother M. Philothea, F.C.S.P.							X	X	X	X	X		
Mother M. Rose Elizabeth, C.S.C.							X	X	X				
Mother M. Regina, R.S.M.								X	X	X	X	X	X
Sister Elizabeth Ann, I.H.M.								X	X				
Sister Thomas Aquinas, R.S.M.								X	X	X			
Mother Catherine, D.C.										X	X	X	
Mother Kathryn Marie, C.S.C.										X	X	X	
Sister Annette Walters, C.S.J.											X	X	
#Chairperson 1954-57													
##Vice-chairperson 1954-57													

CONFERENCE OFFICERS
SFC-CMSW COMMITTEE

	'54	'55	'56	'57	'58	'59	'60	'61	'62	'63	'64	'65	'66
CONFERENCE OFFICERS													
National Chairman													
Mother M. Philothea, F.C.S.P.				X	X								
Mother Catherine, D.C.						X	X	X					
Mother Regina, R.S.M.									X	X			
National Vice-Chairman													
Mother M. Rose Elizabeth, C.S.C.				X	X	X							
Mother Regina, R.S.M.							X	X					
Mother Kathryn Marie, C.S.C.									X	X			
Editor, SF Bulletin													
Sister Ritamary, C.H.M.	X	X	X	X	X	X	X	X	X	X	X		
Inservice Coordinator													
Sister Elizabeth Ann, I.H.M.				X	X	X		X	X				
Executive Secretary													
Sister Mary Emil, I.H.M.				X	X	X							
Sister Annette, C.S.J.							X	X	X	X	X		
Mission Project													
Sister Mary Josetta, R.S.M.							X	X					
Director of Special Projects													
Sister Paul Joseph, I.H.M.								X					
Community Consultant													
Sister Mary Emil, I.H.M.									X				
Sister Rose Dominic, S.C.L.										X			
Overseas Project													
Sister Mary Josetta, R.S.M.									X	X			
Permanent Vice-Chairman													
Sister Mary Emil, I.H.M.										X			
	'54	'55	'56	'57	'58	'59	'60	'61	'62	'63	'64	'65	'66
SFC-CMSWI Committee													
Mother M. Regina, I.H.M.						X	X						
Sister Elizabeth Carmelita, S.N.D.						X	X						
Mother M. Mark, S.N.J.M.						X	X						
Mother M. Amata, C.D.P.								X	X	X			
Mother M. Justin, O.P.								X	X	X			
Mother M. Pacis, I.H.M.								X	X				
Mother M. Florence, S.L.										X			

EVERETT WORKSHOP PARTICIPANTS

Sister Educators:

- Sister Emmanuel, OSF: Dean, College of St. Teresa, Winona, Minnesota; English and literature
- Sister Jerome, OSB: Dean, Donnelly College, Kansas City; Kansas: modern and classical languages
- Sister Thomas Albert, OP: Albertus Magnus College, New Haven, Connecticut; political science and sociology
- Sister Mary, SL: Loretto Heights College, Denver, Colorado; history
- Sister M. Xaveria, IHM: Marygrove College, Monroe, Michigan: mathematics
- Sister Rose Emanuella, SNJM: Dean, College of the Holy Names, Oakland, California; philosophy
- Sister Mary Emil, IHM: Marygrove College, Monroe, Michigan; philosophy
- Sister Jean Marie, SSND: Mount Mary College, Milwaukee, Wisconsin; theology
- Sister Thomasine, OP: Rosary College, Chicago, Illinois; economics
- Sister Barbara, SC: Mount St. Joseph College, Cincinnati, Ohio; psychology
- Sister Mary Marguerite Christine, BVM: Mundelein College, Chicago, Illinois; physical science
- Sister M. Liguori, SCL: St. Mary College, Xavier, Kansas; biology
- Sister M. Augustine, OSF: President, Alverno College, Milwaukee, Wisconsin; education
- Sister Judith, FCSP: Mount St. Vincent, Seattle, Washington; education
- Sister Elizabeth Ann, IHM: Immaculate Heart College, Los Angeles, California; education

Consultants to the Workshop:

- Dr. T. M. Stinnett: Executive Secretary of the National Commmission on Teacher Education and Professional Standards
- Father R.J. Henle, SJ: Dean, Graduate School, St. Louis Unviersity
- Dr. Russell M. Cooper: Assistant Dean, College of Science, Literature and the Arts, University of Minnesota
- Dr. John O. Riedl: Graduate Dean, Marquette University
- Rev. John J. Flanagan: Director, Catholic Hospital Association

- Sister Esther, SP: St. Mary of the Woods College
- Sister Bertrande, DC: Marillac Seminary, St. Louis, Missouri

The institutional observers from the two institutions chosen as demonstration centers for the Everett curriculum:

College of St. Teresa, Winona, Minnesota

- Sister Ancina, OSF
- Sister M. Romana, OSF
- Sister M. Yolande, OSF
- Sister M. Laura, OSF

St. Vincent, Seattle, Washington

- Sister Elizabeth Clare, FCSP
- Sister Marie Carmen, FCSP
- Sister Mary Claver, FCSP

THE EVERETT CURRICULUM DEMONSTRATION CENTERS

The College of Saint Teresa

For fifty years, the College of Saint Teresa, operated by the Sisters of St. Francis, had served as an educational institution for lay women. For many years it had also served the needs of sisters, their own and those of other communities. With an extension campus on the motherhouse grounds, it had been possible for the sisters in formation to attend classes in a reflective setting. Since the community had varied apostolates, the curriculum plan was a sequence of courses whereby all sisters regardless of their profession could share common backgrounds in theology, philosophy, and general education. This general education allowed the sister to be a liberally educated person and to lay the foundation for future specialization or graduate work.

> The young religious stays there [motherhouse, Rochester, MN] from her postulancy until she makes her first vows. The novitiate school is the branch campus of the College. The members of the faculty are members of the faculty of the College of Saint Teresa. At the end of the second year novitiate, the novice takes her first vows and comes to the College of Saint Teresa where she remains for two years in the juniorate under the direction of the junior mistress. She completes the work in her major and minor fields in college and receives her degree before she is sent into the schools to teach or to take up her occupation in the community.[1]

The sister attended separate classes while at the branch campus but once back at the main campus she took classes, except for theology and philosophy, with the lay students. Four aims for sister education were the basis for Saint Teresa's joining the experiment. First, the primary goal of the educational program should be the development of the person who is a sister.

This meant thinking of an undergraduate program which would interpenetrate and complement the other spiritual and psychological experiences in her religious formation and bring to it an intellectual understanding that would make the demands of religious life more meaningful and valuable.

Secondly, it was hoped that all sisters would come to share a common basis of liberal education that would allow them to live more effectively a common life since all would have a common core of knowledge. It was also recognized that a wider range of knowledge was necessary for the demands of today. The greater exposure also allowed the sister the facility to change easily from one grade or subject level to another.

Thirdly, it was believed that all sisters, especially those going into teacher education, should have a subject area concentration. A sister was to come to know enough in one field of knowledge to feel competent in that field. This sense of competency, it was hoped, would give the sister a personal security, engendering, in turn, better mental health and a sense of morale. Such a specialization would also help to add variety to a house of sisters where a sharing of various talents would make for a "collegium" effect. Lastly, it was hoped that sisters would receive enough professional preparation to have the skills and experience to meet the demands of teaching.

Providence Heights

The general plan for Providence Heights was to provide a college for sisters taught by sisters. The first faculty was to be made up of ten members, each responsible for one, perhaps two, departments.

> Since the Bergeron Providence Demonstration Center[2] is being planned and worked out from an absolute beginning as it were, and since the first faculty members are now being trained, it will be necessary to teach the Everett Curriculum for a period of at least four years with Seattle University. A special feature of the project, however, will consist of requesting the University to teach, to administer this program as a separate curriculum within the arts college, to organize separate classes for the Providence Sisters, and to teach the courses in the order and according to the plan worked out in the Everett pattern. The Seattle University professors who are asked to cooperate with this program for these first few years will not of course be as closely identified with it as the Sister teachers who are being prepared for it, but it is felt that the four years' experience in teaching the curriculum inside the University with professors of varying backgrounds will yield a great deal of experimental data which can be put to good use when the program begins to operate as a separate center.[3]

Ideally, the Everett Curriculum was to be implemented on a campus only for sisters. Because of the time it would take to train a faculty to the doctoral level and in order to implement the Everett Curriculum as soon as possible, Seattle University consented to cooperate with the plan by using its faculty and establishing a separate unit within the University. There were actually two plans: the interim and the regular one. The interim program worked around the sister students occupying temporary buildings until those planned were built. While sister faculty were being trained, select university professors began to put the Everett curriculum into practice. The Providence Center was to be an institutional branch of the university. Under the regular program, the sisters would be residing on their own campus in specially designed buildings that included a library and laboratory facilities. The faculty were trained to the doctoral level. It was felt that the interim level would last for five years with another five years needed to evaluate the situation.

Several results were anticipated from this plan. The same basic liberal education would be offered to all sisters regardless of their professional field. Emphasis on the behavioral sciences was to affect the lives of the students due to the integrative factors involved. Professional requirements came at the end of the educational experience. New approaches were taken to accomplish student teaching work. Finally, the cultural life of the student was enriched by a planned co-curriculum. All this depended on whether state certification requirements could be worked out.

> The college was located on a two hundred forty-three acre site at Pine Lake, near Issaquah, fifteen miles east of Seattle, Washington, and was known as Providence Heights College. Constructed at a cost of six million dollars, the campus had nine buildings and was able to handle an enrollment of three hundred sisters. It served as the Sister Formation College of Seattle University, and its curriculum followed the Everett plan. Ten faculty members designated for the new school were sent to study at several universities. The unique plan was to include the fact that all faculty members were to hold doctoral degrees. Announced as the nation's first college devoted totally to the intellectual, spiritual and professional formation of sisters, it was rather the first four-year, all-sisters' college within a university. The staff and student body came from four religious communities, and the program of studies was planned jointly by participating orders and Seattle University. The Sisters of Charity of Providence coordinated the policies and assigned a dean of studies. The four religious communities of women joined in this new venture were: Sisters of Charity of Providence, Seattle; Sisters of St. Joseph of Newark, New Jersey; Dominican Sisters of the Congregation of the Holy Cross, Amityville, New York and the

Dominican Sisters of the Congregation of St. Thomas Aquinas, Tacoma, Washington.[4]

The dedication of the college took place on July 21, 1961 with the apostolic delegate to the United States, Bishop Egidio Vagnozzi, and eight bishops and archbishops from the western United States and Alaska presiding. The sisters of the various communities signed an agreement that detailed the arrangements for this educational endeavor. Part of the agreement stated that the communities would agree to:

> . . . follow the Everett Curriculum strictly in its philosophy and its detailed provisions, and to make no departure from it not authorized by the curriculum committee of the College of Sister Formation and no essential departure from it not authorized by the Curriculum committee of the College of Sister Formation and approved by the Academic Council of the University.[5]

Along with this strict adherence to the Everett Curriculum was the agreement that after 1965 no sister teacher would be allowed to teach at Providence Heights without a doctoral degree. An inter-community sister faculty was established along with Jesuit faculty members. The sisters of the faculty were also encouraged to teach one course every year to the lay students on the university campus and at other off-campus centers of Providence Heights College. All degrees for Sisters were awarded and conferred by Seattle University with the recommendation of the Dean of the College of Sister Formation.

The curriculum fulfilled college requirements with emphasis on a sequence of behavioral sciences and contemporary affairs, courses related to the human person, sequences in philosophy and theology, psychology and social sciences and professional education. The program extended over at least four years with the additional year for professional training.

Believing that training should take place first on the level of general courses and only then on to specialized areas, this curriculum was devised in such a way that the sister would not specialize until a complete sequence of general education work had been accomplished. It was also decided that the work of specializing would more than likely take place on the level of graduate education or within a fifth year of undergraduate work. The basic curriculum was built on two sequences that balanced one another: philosophy and theology. Philosophy was taught first and became a rational basis for the study of theology. Theology was to be taught as a discipline and not as a group of facts.

The field of concentration was to be in the area of behavioral sciences. Included in this area were closely knit sequences in philosophy, biology, psychology, the social sciences, history and geography. It was believed that prepared in this way, the teacher would be able to deal effectively with others and at the same time be more aware of the human environment in which she lived.

Professional education courses were divided between the areas of school curriculum, educational foundations, and student teaching. Always it was the aim that knowledge be related to action. In order to relate knowledge to action, certain humanistic elements were consciously introduced at appropriate places in the study of the social sciences. In this way, it was possible to bring the student to a realization that what she was studying was not merely theoretical, but was related to basic human values.

Spiritual formation was seen as including adequate instruction in theology, intense living of the doctrine of the Mystical Body, and learning through the example of others. Intellectual formation was to cover a liberal education resulting in the ability and skill needed for her professional level, and original and critical thinking. Professional formation was to grant a mastery in the field of her profession, a curiosity and a desire for research. Social-physical formation was to help the sister understand her physical and emotional makeup and acquire a sense of balance between work and prayer, silence and recreation. The integration of these objectives in a proper sequence of courses and instruction was a constant object of evaluation. Even the functions of the instructors were explored. Overall, the college was exploring how a sister could grow in the intellectual life and in holiness.

NOTES

CHAPTER I

1. David J. O'Brien, "Needed: A 'New' History," *America*, 3 May 1969, 528-529.

2. Sister Joan Chittister, OSB, *Winds of Change* (Kansas City: Sheed and Ward, 1986), 122.

3. Sister Elizabeth Kolmer, ASC, *Religious Women in the United States* (Delaware: Michael Glazier, Inc., 1984), 13.

4. Courtois Abbe Gaston, comp., *The States of Perfection* (Westminster, MD: The Newman Press, 1961), 472.

5. Sister Mary Emil Penet, IHM, to Sister Bertrande Meyers, DC, 21 April 1956, Department of Special Collections and University Archives, Marquette University, Milwaukee, Wisconsin, The Sister Formation Conference/Religious Formation Conference Archives (hereafter cited as SFC Archives).

6. Sister Josetta Butler, RSM, interview with author, Chicago, Illinois, September 1986.

7. Butler, interview.

8. Sister Madeleva Wolff, CSC, *My First Seventy Years* (New York: The Macmillan Company, 1959), 111-112.

9. *National Catholic Educational Association Bulletin, Proceedings and Addresses, Forty-Fifth Annual Meeting*, (Washington, DC: National Catholic Education Association, 1948), 213.

10. *National Catholic Educational Association Bulletin, Proceedings and Addresses, Forty-Fifth Annual Meeting*, Sister M. Madeleva, "The Education of our Young Religious Teachers," 253-256.

11. *National Catholic Educational Association Bulletin, Proceedings and Addresses, Forty-Sixth Annual Meeting*, (Washington, DC: National Catholic Educational Association, 1949), 255.

12. Wolff, *My First Seventy Years*, 113.

13. *National Catholic Educational Association Bulletin, Proceedings and Addresses, Forty-Sixth Annual Meeting*, Brother Emilian, FSC, "Teacher Training in Seminary and Scholasticate," 272.

14. *National Catholic Educational Association Bulletin, Proceedings and Addresses, Forty-Seventh Annual Meeting,* (Washington, DC: National Catholic Educational Association, 1950), 213.

15. *National Catholic Educational Association Bulletin, Proceedings and Addresses, Forty-Eighth Annual Meeting,* (Washington, DC: National Catholic Educational Association, 1951), 163.

16. Sister Xaveria Barton, IHM, interview with author, Monroe, Michigan, September 1986.

17. *National Catholic Educational Association Bulletin, Proceedings and Addresses, Forty-Ninth Annual Meeting,* (Washington, DC: National Catholic Educational Association, 1952), 203.

18. Sister Mary Emil Penet, IHM, Notes to the Sisters, date unknown, SFC Archives.

19. Survey on Teacher-Preparation, 1952, SFC Archives.

20. Barton, interview.

21. Brother William Mang, CSC, to Sister Mary Richardine Quirk, BVM, 16 February 1954, SFC Archives.

22. Survey on Teacher-Preparation, 1952, SFC Archives.

23. Survey on Teacher-Preparation, 1952, SFC Archives.

24. Butler, interview.

25. Sister Bertrande Meyers, DC, *Sisters for the 21st Century* (New York: Sheed and Ward, 1965), 107.

26. Cardinal Samuel Stritch to Sister Mary Richardine Quirk, BVM, 29 August 1952, SFC Archives.

27. Msgr. F. N. Pitt to Sister Mary Richardine Quick, BVM, 8 January 1953, SFC Archives.

28. Msgr. F. N. Pitt to Sister Mary Richardine Quick, BVM, 17 February 1953, SFC Archives.

29. Informal Talk of Sister Mary Emil Penet, IHM, to her Sisters, unknown date, SFC Archives.

30. Msgr. McManus to Sister Mary Richardine Quirk, BVM, 18 May 1953, SFC Archives.

31. Sister Mary Richardine Quirk, BVM, to Rev. Paul Philippe, OP, 2 January 1955, SFC Archives.

32. Msgr. Pitt to Sister Mary Richardine Quirk, BVM, 9 March 1953, SFC Archives.

33. *National Catholic Educational Association Bulletin, Proceedings and Addresses, Fiftieth Annual Meeting,* (Washington, DC: National Catholic Educational Association, 1953), 223.

34. Informal Talk of Sister Mary Emil Penet, IHM, to her Sisters.

35. Sister Mary Emil Penet, IHM, "The Sisters' View," 1953, SFC Archives.

36. Informal Talk of Sister Mary Emil Penet, IHM, to her Sisters.

37. *National Catholic Educational Association Bulletin, Proceedings and Addresses, Fiftieth Annual Meeting,* 220.

38. Sister Mary Emil Penet, IHM, Notes to the Sisters, date unknown.

39. Penet, Notes to the Sisters.

40. Sister Mary Emil Penet, IHM, Informal Talk to her Sisters.

41. Penet, Notes to the Sisters.

42. Penet, Notes to the Sisters.

43. Penet, Notes to the Sisters.

44. Penet, Notes to the Sisters.

45. Sister Mary Richardine Quirk, BVM, to Msgr. McManus, 26 March 1954, SFC Archives.

46. Minutes of NCEA Executive Board Meeting, Lake Placid, New York, 19 June 1953, SFC Archives.

47. Sister Ritamary Bradley, CHM, ed., *Sister Formation Bulletin,* Official Publication of the Sister Formation Conference (Milwaukee: Marquette University Press, 1959), "Why The Sister Formation Bulletin?", 1.1.3.*

48. Sister Mary Emil Penet, IHM, "The Role of Catholic Higher Education in the Preparation of Teachers for Catholic Schools," 20 April 1954, SFC Archives.

49. Barton, interview.

50. Sister Ritamary Bradley, interview with author, Davenport, Iowa, September 1986.

*For all following similar endnotes, read first number as volume, second as issue, and third as page.

CHAPTER II

1. Meyers, *Sisters for the 21st Century,* 108.

2. Sister Ritamary Bradley, CHM, ed., *The Mind of the Church in the Formation of Sisters,* (New York: Fordham University Press, 1956), xxxi.

3. See chart in the appendix for membership of Sister Formation Conference National Committees from 1954-1966.

4. Sister Mary Emil Penet, IHM, to the members of the National Consultative Committee, Sister Formation Conference, 29 June 1954, SFC Archives.

5. Meyers, *Sisters for the 21st Century*, p. 116.

6. Bradley, ed., *The Mind of the Church in the Formation of Sisters,* 61.

7. Bradley, interview.

8. Bradley, ed., *Sister Formation Bulletin*, Sister Mary Emil, "Progress Report on Sister Formation," Supplement 1. 2.

9. Sister Mary Emil Penet, IHM, Report, 13 June, 1956, SFC Archives.

10. Minutes of the Meeting of the Sister Formation Committee and Regional Chairmen of Sister Formation Conferences, 12 April, 1955, SFC Archives.

11. There were four published volumes in this series: 1954-55: *The Mind of the Church in the Formation of Sisters*; 1955-56: *Spiritual and Intellectual Elements in the Formation of Sisters*; 1956-57: *Planning for the Formation of Sisters*; 1957-58: *The Juniorate in Sister Formation.*

12. Msgr. Frederick G. Hochwalt, "Sister Formation," *America*, 26 May 1956, 224.

13. Sister Mary Emil Penet, IHM, to Msgr. Hochwalt, 6 November 1954, The Catholic University of America Archives, NCEA Collection.

14. Bradley, ed., *Sister Formation Bulletin*, "Why the Sister Formation Bulletin?", 1.1.3.

15. Sister Mary Emil Penet, IHM, to Msgr. Hochwalt, 29 June 1954, SFC Archives.

16. Penet to Hochwalt.

17. Bradley, ed. *Sister Formation Bulletin*, "SF Bulletin Readership," 3.2.24.

18. Sister Mary Emil Penet, IHM, Statement, unknown date, SFC Archives.

19. Summary of Responses to Questionnaires on Sister Formation, 20 December 1955, SFC Archives.

20. Bradley, ed., *Sister Formation Bulletin*, Sister Mary Emil, "Progress Report on Sister Formation," Supplement I, Summer 1956, 2.

21. Bradley, ed., *Sister Formation Bulletin*, "Report on SFC Committee Meeting," 2.3.14.

22. Cardinal Arcadio Larraona, CMF, to Father Edwin Quain, 22 May 1957, SFC Archives.

23. *National Catholic Education Bulletin, Proceedings and Addresses, Fifty-Third Annual Meeting,* (Washington, DC: National Catholic Educational Association, 1956), 45.

24. Sister Mary Emil Penet, IHM, to Members of the NSFC and Regional Chairmen, 9 November 1956, SFC Archives.

25. Bradley, ed., *Sister Formation Bulletin*, "A Decree Giving Norms For Conventions Which Deal With Adaptation and Renovation In The States of Perfection," 3.1.19.

26. Minutes of the Meeting of the National Executive Committee for Women Religious of the United States, 9 April 1956, University of Notre Dame Archives, LCWR Files.

27. Sister Margaret Mary Modde, OSF, "A Canonical Study of the Leadership Conference of Women Religious of the United States of America" (Ph.D. diss. Catholic University of America, 1977), 111-112.

28. Bradley, ed., *Sister Formation Bulletin*, "New National Group Organized," 3.2.12.

29. Sister Mary Emil Penet, IHM, to SF Committee and Regional Chairmen, 15 December 1956, Sister of Providence Archives.

30. Butler, Interview.

31. Dr. T. M. Stinnett to Sister Mary Emil Penet, IHM, date unknown, SFC Archives.

32. Meyers, *Sisters for the 21st Century*, 110.

33. Bradley, ed., *Sister Formation Bulletin*, Sister Mary Emil, "The Sister Formation Movement And The Pastoral Outlook," 1.2.3.

34. *National Catholic Educational Bulletin, Proceedings and Addresses, Fifty-Third Annual Meeting*, 49-50.

CHAPTER III

1. Sister Mary Emil Penet, IHM, ed., *Report of Everett Curriculum Workshop* (Seattle: Heiden's Mailing Bureau, September 1956), 18.

2. Sister Mary Emil Penet, IHM, "Everett Workshop and Nursing Education," 1962, SFC Archives.

3. Barton, interview.

4. Informal minutes of the Everett Workshop, 12 June, 1956, SFC Archives.

5. Sister M. Emmanuel Collins, OSF, Report, "Symposium: The Everett Story," date unknown, SFC Archives.

6. Penet, ed., *Report of Everett Curriculum Workshop*, 6.

7. Informal Report to Sister Formation Faculty on Appraisal of Sister Formation Program, 8 March 1960, Providence Heights College of Sister Formation, Issaquah, WA Collection, Sisters of Providence Archives, Seattle, Washington.

8. Informal Everett Workshop Minutes, 6 June 1956, Sisters of Providence Archives. "Sister Emmanuel gave a report of her study of standards and patterns

of sister education in Europe. During the period of 1 October 1955 to May 1956 she visited schools and convents in England, France, Germany and Italy. Sister expalined [sic] the conditions of Catholic education in each of these countries. Among the many newer developments in Catholic education she highlighted the programs of the Institute Catholique of Paris, the Maria SS. Assunta and the Regina Mundi, international college for sisters at Rome. In discussing the sisters she described their status in the European society and the problems they encounter in the work of sister formation."

9. A listing of the Everett participants is in the appendix.

10. Sister Mary Emil Penet, IHM, to the Sisters, 1 September 1955, SFC Archives.

11. Sister Mary Emil Penet, IHM, to the Sisters, 22 October 1955, SFC Archives.

12. Penet to the Sisters.

13. Proposed Study and Curriculum Project: A Memorandum for Dr. Eurich, The Catholic University of America Archives, Washington, DC, National Catholic Education Association Collection, date unknown.

14. Proposed Study and Curriculum Project, 1.

15. Penet, ed., *Report of Everett Curriculum Workshop*, 18, 23.

16. Sister Mary Emil Penet, IHM, Talk, 13 June 1956, SFC Archives.

17. Informal Minutes of the Everett Workshop, 4 June 1956, SFC Archives.

18. Sister Mary Emil Penet, IHM, to the Members of the National Consultative Committee, and the National Sister Formation Committee, 7 June 1956, SFC Archives.

19. Sister Mary Emil Penet, IHM, to the Sisters, 7 June 1956, SFC Archives.

20. Sister Mary Emil Penet, IHM, Informal report, date unknown, SFC Archives.

21. More information on the College of Saint Teresa and Providence Heights can be found in the appendix. The absence of serious study of Marillac College, St. Louis, Missouri, in this work was due to the fact that it was not an official Everett Curriculum Demonstration Center.

22. Penet, ed., *Report of Everett Curriculum Workshop*, 126.

23. Bradley, ed., *Planning for the Formation of Sisters*, xiv.

24. Sister Elizabeth Ann, IHM, "Cost Differentials and Sources of Revenue in the Expansion of the Parochial Schools," and Sister Rose Matthew, IHM, "Sister Teachers in the United States: A Study of Their Status and Projected Role," and "Sister Teachers in the United States: A Study of Their Status and Projected Role," SFC Archives.

25. Sister Ritamary Bradley, CHM, ed., *Planning for the Formation of Sisters*, (New York: Fordham University Press, 1957), 13.

26. Chittister, *Winds of Change*, 123.

CHAPTER IV

1. Sister Mary Emil Penet, IHM, Talk to the Forty-First Annual Convention of Catholic Hospital Associations, 24 May 1956, SFC Archives.

2. *National Catholic Educational Association Bulletin, Proceedings and Addresses, Fifty-Fourth Annual Meeting,* (Washington, DC: National Catholic Educational Association, 1957), 112.

3. *National Catholic Educational Bulletin, Proceedings and Addresses Fifty-Fourth Annual Meeting,* 112.

4. Sister Cecile Lechner, SCC, interview with author, Mendham, New Jersey, September 1986.

5. Bradley, ed., *Sister Formation Bulletin,* Sister Mary Emil, "Why A Juniorate?" 7.1.10.

6. Sister Ritamary Bradley, CHM, Paper, "Responsibility of the Sister Today," unknown date, SFC Archives.

7. Sister Ritamary Bradley, CHM, ed., *The Juniorate,* (New York: Fordham University Press, 1960), 6.

8. Minutes of the Meeting of the Executive Committee for Women Religious of the United States of America, 9 September 1956, Notre Dame University Archives, LCWR Collection.

9. Bradley, ed., *The Juniorate,* the foreword by Arcadio Cardinal Larraona.

10. Bradley, ed., *The Juniorate,* the forword.

11. Sister Mary Emil Penet, IHM, to the National Sister Formation Committee and Regional Chairmen, 4 March 1958, SFC Archives.

12. Sister Ritamary Bradley, CHM, to Sister Mary Emil Penet, IHM, 3 August 1958, SFC Archives.

13. Sister M. Lelia, DC, Paper, "Time in Regard to the Juniorate," 7 May 1959, SFC Archives.

14. Bradley, ed., *Sister Formation Bulletin,* Mother Mary Consolatrice, BVM, "The In-Service Sister and the Problem of Time: What Can the Higher Superior Do?" 5.2.14.

15. *National Catholic Educational Association Bulletin Proceedings and Addresses, Fifty-Sixth Annual Meeting,* (Washington, DC: National Catholic Educational Association, 1959), 161.

16. Sister Emmanuel Collins, OSF, interview with author, Rochester, Minnesota, November 1986.

17. Butler, interview.

18. Sister Mary Emil Penet, IHM, to Sister Mary Richardine Quirk, BVM, 30 September 1957, SFC Archives.

19. Sister Elizabeth Ann, IHM, to Sisters, Spring 1958, SFC Archives.

20. Sister Elizabeth Ann, IHM, to Sisters.

21. Bradley, interview.

22. Father Elio Gambari, SMM, "The Task of the Sisters who Teach Religious," Marquette Workshop 1960, SFC Archives.

23. Bradley, ed., *Sister Formation Bulletin*, "Marquette Workshop Proposes Policy Statements" 7.1.13.

24. "The Second Workshop in Instructional Programs in Spirituality," August 1960, SFC Archives.

25. Bradley, ed., *Sister Formation Bulletin*, Letter, Valerio Cardinal Valeri to Sister Mary Emil Penet, IHM, 31 October 1959. 6.2.10.

26. Bradley, ed., *The Juniorate,* Reverend Elio Gambari, SMM, "The Juniorate in the Mind and Directives of the Holy See," 2.

27. Cardinal Arcadio Larraona to Rev. Paul Reinert, SJ, 13 April 1957, "Sister Formation Conference: Correspondence, Newsletters, Minutes"; Leadership Conference of Women Religious Collection, CLCW 34/14; University of Notre Dame Archives.

28. Cardinal Arcadio Larraona to Mother Alcuin, OSF, 23 June 1958, SFC Archives.

29. Memo on Executive Committee of the Higher Superiors Conference, 1958, SFC Archives.

30. Sister Mary Emil Penet, IHM, to Mother Mary Maurice, RSM, 9 September 1958, SFC Archives.

31. Sister Mary Emil Penet, IHM, to Mother Philothea, FCSP, undated, SFC Archives.

32. Memorandum on Sister Formation Conference presented to the American Bishops by Msgr. Hochwalt, 1959, SFC Archives.

33. Butler, interview.

34. Report of the Sister Formation Meeting, 26-28 August 1958, SFC Archives.

35. Sister Richardine Quirk, BVM, "The Evolution of the Idea of Sister Formation, 1952-1960," *Sponsa Regis,* April 1962, 232.

CHAPTER V

1. Bradley, ed., *Sister Formation Bulletin*, foreword, vii. 1.1-4.4.

2. Sister Margaret Ann McNamara, SP, "The Emerging Role of American Women Religious in the Catholic Church," *Sisters Today*, 13.

3. Kolmer, *Religious Women in the United States*, 41.

4. Kolmer, 41.

5. Leon Joseph Cardinal Suenens, *The Nun in the World* (Maryland: The Newman Press, 1963), 33.

6. Albert E. Meder, Jr. of Middle States Association of Colleges and Secondary Schools to Msgr. Alfred F. Horrigan, 28 June 1963, SFC Archives.

7. William K. Selden, National Commission on Accreditation, to Father Dunne, 19 November 1962, SFC Archives.

8. Butler, interview.

9. Resume of Seminar for Administration of Sisters' Colleges, 13-24 June 1963, SFC Archives.

10. Bradley, ed., *Sister Formation Bulletin*, "Sister Formation Leadership Meeting," 9.1.19.

11. Sister Annette Walters, CSJ, to Msgr. Shannon, 15 December 1962, SFC Archives.

12. Sister Mary Emil Penet, IHM, to Father D'Souza, 17 April 1959, SFC Archives.

13. Bradley, ed., *Sister Formation Bulletin,* 7.3.6.

14. Bradley, ed., *Sister Formation Bulletin,* 7.3.6.

15. Sister Annette Walters, CSJ, to Father Gambari, 8 June 1963, SFC Archives.

16. *National Catholic Educational Association Bulletin, Proceedings and Address, Sixty-First Annual Meeting,* (Washington, DC National Catholic Educational Association, 1964). Father Matthew Ahmann "Understanding the Interracial Question: An Element in Sister Formation," 178-179.

17. Report of the Sister Formation Conference to the Executive Committee of the Conference of Major Superiors of Women's Institutes of the United States, 26 February 1964, SFC Archives.

18. Sister Betty Carroll, RSM, phone interview with author,10 July 1985.

19. Sister Roberta Rorke, SP, Sister Formation Research Study, 1977, Providence Heights College of Sister Formation, Issaquah, WA Collection, Sisters of Providence Archives, Seattle, Washington.

20. Sister Annette Walters, CSJ, to Brother Leo Ryan, CSV, 17 October 1962, SFC Archives.

21. Bradley, interview.

22. News Release, 12 August 1963, SFC Archives.

23. Outline for Institute for Juniorate Studies, SFC Archives.

24. Francois Houtart, *The Challenge to Change: The Church Confronts the Future*, ed., Mary Anne Chouteau (New York: Sheed and Ward, 1964), preface.

25. Sister Annette Walters, CSJ, to United States Bishops, August 1964, SFC Archives.

26. Bradley, ed., *Sister Formation Bulletin*, "Report of Leadership Meeting," 7.1.15.

27. Proposal to Raskob Foundation, 7 January 1959, SFC Archives.

28. "Current Comment," *America*, 5 May 1962, 195.

29. *National Catholic Educational Association Bulletin, Proceedings and Addresses, Fifty-Eighth Annual Meeting,* (Washington, DC: National Catholic Educational Association, 1961), 145.

30. Sister Annette Walters, CSJ, to Monsignor Hochwalt, 2 November 1960, SFC Archives.

31. Report to the Raskob Foundation, 31 December 1962, SFC Archives.

32. Draft, "A Petition for Aid to Establish A Program of Education in Nursing on a New Level in Order to Provide Broader Foundations for Leadership Positions," SFC Archives.

33. Questionnaire on the Mission Project, Marquette, October 1960, SFC Archives.

34. Sister Annette Walters, CSJ, to Mother Mary Consolatrice, BVM, 16 June 1960, SFC Archives.

35. Sister Annette Walters, CSJ, to Mother Mary Consolatrice, BVM, 22 November 1961, SFC Archives.

36. Mother Mary Consolatrice, BVM, to Sister Annette Walters, CSJ, 25 February 1962, SFC Archives.

37. Sister Annette Walters, CSJ, to Father Gambari, 12 September 1962, SFC Archives.

38. Cardinal Arcadio Larraona to Mother Alcuin, OSF, 23 June 1958, SFC Archives.

39. Sister Annette Walters, CSJ, to Father Gambari, 12 September 1962, SFC Archives.

40. Minutes, 29 August 1963 CMSW Meeting, SFC Archives.

41. Sister Annette Walters, CSJ, to the Sister Formation Conference Leadership Group, 2 September 1963, SFC Archives.

42. Mother Mary Consolatrice, BVM, to the Hierarchy, the Major Superiors of Women, the Superintendents of Schools, the Consultative Committee of Sister Formation and the Sister Formation Committee, 6 September 1963, SFC Archives.

43. Mother Mary Regina, RSM, to the Mothers and Sisters, 8 October 1963, SFC Archives.

44. Mother Mary Regina, RSM, to Mothers General, 21 October 1963, SFC Archives.

45. Sister M. Emmanuel Collins, OSF, to Father Gambari, 12 November 1963, SFC Archives.

46. Sister Annette Walters, CSJ, open letter, October 1964, SFC Archives.

47. Sister Mary Emil Penet, IHM, to Mother Mary Regina, RSM, 6 March 1964, SFC Archives.

48. Msgr. Hochwalt to Mother M. Gemma, OSB, 25 September 1964, The Catholic University of America Archives, NCEA Collection.

49. Sister Annette Walters, CSJ, open letter, October 1964, SFC Archives.

50. Minutes, 29 August 1963 CMSW Meeting, SFC Archives.

51. Minutes, CMSW Meeting.

52. Collins, interview.

53. Sister Annette Walters, CSJ, open letter, October 1964, SFC Archives.

54. Bradley, interview.

55. Report of the Sister Formation Conference to the Executive Committee of the Conference of Major Superiors of Women's Institutes of the United States, 26 February 1964, SFC Archives.

CHAPTER VI

1. David O'Brien, *The Renewal of American Catholicism* (New York: Oxford University Press, 1972), 37.

2. O'Brien, *The Renewal of American Catholicism*, 21.

3. O'Brien, *The Renewal of American Catholicism*, 22.

4. Martin Marty, Stuart Rosenberg, and Andrew Greeley, *What Do We Believe?* (New York: Meredith Press, 1968), 124.

5. Houtart, *The Challenge to Change: The Church Confronts the Future,* 8.

6. Ann Patrick Ware, ed., *Midwives of the Future,* Elizabeth Carroll, "Reaping the Fruits of Redemption," (Kansas City, Missouri: Leaven Press, 1985), 59.

7. Chittister, *Winds of Change,* 122.

8. Robert De Board, *The Psychoanalysis of Organizations,* (London: Tavistock, 1978), 39-42.

9. Donald N. Levine, ed., *George Simmel On Individuality and Social Forms,* (Chicago: University of Chicago Press, 1971), 348.

10. Chittister, *Winds of Change,* 124.

11. Mary Daly, *The Church and the Second Sex,* (New York: Harper & Row, 1975), 36.

12. Kolmer, *Religious Women in the United States,* 78.

13. Mary Jo Weaver, *New Catholic Women: A contemporary Challenge to Traditional Religious Authority,* (San Francisco: Harper & Row, 1985), 89.

14. Kolmer, *Religious Women in the United States,* 78.

APPENDIX D

1.   Sister M. Emmanuel Collins, OSF, to Mr. Robert A. Broenen, News Editor of The Catholic Bulletin, 1 August 1960, SFC Archives.

2.   The Providence Demonstration Center was at first called Bergeron, after a piece of land near Everett, Washington.

3.   Informal Minutes of the Everett Workshop, 13 August 1956, SFC Archives.

4.   News Release, Sister Formation Conference, 29 September 1958, SFC Archives.

5.   Agreement Between Seattle University and Religious Communities, 1960, SFC Archives.

ABOUT THE AUTHOR

MARJORIE NOTERMAN BEANE, PH.D.

Dr. Marjorie Noterman Beane is an inspiration to Catholic education. Her dedication to Catholicism and to the history of the American woman religious has made her a leader in the field of education. Dr. Beane exhibits an extensive list of scholastic achievements and contributions.

With undergraduate degrees from Mallinckrodt College and Marillac College, a master of education degree from University of Arizona and a doctorate degree from Loyola University of Chicago, Dr. Beane possesses a strong background in the liberal arts, history and educational administration. She is recognized for her achievements through listings in *Who's Who of Emerging Leaders in America*, *Who's Who of American Women*, *Who's Who in American Education* and Oxford's *Who's Who*.

Dr. Beane's scholastic contributions are also very impressive. They include filling a variety of roles in elementary, secondary and higher education. In 1969, Dr. Beane began her distinguished career in education as a teacher at St. Alphonsus School in Prospect Heights, Illinois. She taught at several other Catholic schools in Illinois and was principal at St. Theresa School in Palatine, Illinois from 1975 to 1984.

Dr. Beane began her tenure in higher education in 1984 when she was named vice president for academic affairs and development at Mallinckrodt College. In 1986 she became the College's ninth president. She was instrumental in the 1991 merger of Loyola University of Chicago and Mallinckrodt when the latter became the Mallinckrodt campus of Loyola. She is currently the associate vice president for programmatic development at Loyola University of Chicago where she has served since 1991.

Her educational experiences have taken her to such international destinations as France, Italy, Germany, Jordan, Israel, Greece and Egypt.

Having been a woman religious for many years, Dr. Beane continues her devotion to Catholic education through research on the educational history of the American woman religious.